DECORATION

U.S.A.

DECORATION U.S.A.

by José Wilson

and

Arthur Leaman

THE MACMILLAN COMPANY, NEW YORK / COLLIER-MACMILLAN LIMITED, LONDON

FRONTISPIECE
Arthur Witthoefft, *Architect*
Eleanor Witthoefft, *Designer*

Book designed by Jacqueline Brunet

SECOND PRINTING

To

ELSIE DE WOLFE

who put American decorating on the map

Contents

COLOR PLATES

Winglike roof on a house in Puerto Rico.

Cliff-hanging house in California.

Ground-hugging house in the Middle West.

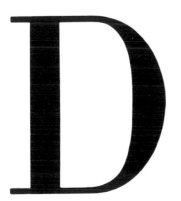

Decoration U.S.A. *is not a book about how to be your own decorator. In the last few years there has been a deluge of books on that subject. It is a documentation and evaluation of the changes that have taken place in America since World War II and their effect on the most personal and recognizable level— the home. If a house is an accurate barometer of the life and times of a people, as archaeologists believe, then the twentieth-century American house will have much to reveal to future generations. Every step up the ladder of progress that has brought more leisure, greater mobility and increased income to the community as a whole has been reflected in the way the people of that community live. A decorating trend originating in Hawaii or California, an architectural innovation from Chicago or New York, quickly spreads across the country. America today is an exciting, exhilarating and frequently bewildering market place of design from excellent to indifferent, and the freedom of choice for the buyer is unparalleled in any other country or century. Herein lies the danger and the challenge. Only a constantly rising level of taste and the ability to recognize and demand the best can prevent this country from becoming, as the direr prophets predict, a wasteland of urban agglomerations and coast-to-coast developments. We believe, on the accumulated evidence of the last twenty years, capsuled in this book, that such taste and ability does exist and*

13

Block-long apartments in Manhattan House, N.Y.C.

Block-high apartments in Marina City, Chicago.

that it will eventually sweep away the mediocre and meaningless in architecture and decoration. As the main motivation for change and improvement we look to the dynamic, daring contemporary architecture which, by altering the shape and purpose of the rooms we live in, has done much to abolish accepted but out-worn decorating clichés. The prevalence of glass and the absence of confining interior walls in many modern houses have affected the forms of furniture, the colors of furnishings, the sources of light and heat and the placement of art and accessories. Yet modern architecure must also be held responsible for some lamentable shortcomings in interiors. The impersonal high-rise apartments with their rigid floor plans and—in the new circular apartment houses—wedge-shaped rooms that have taken over whole blocks in our cities can only be made individual and livable by the reshaping of space through decoration. Less apparent but equally in-fluential, many of the factors that have left their mark on the American scene have their roots in sociology and technology. The mushrooming of second houses and floating homes can be traced to the sprawl of super-highways and the shorter work week. The emergence of the office-at-home may be credited to the growth of super-corporations and their organization men. The big boom in art and music, books and collec-tions is directly attributable to a cultural renaissance on a mass level. With the disappearance of domestic help has come a wave of improvements in kitchens and a less formal style of entertaining that has led to the near-demise of the dining room and a corresponding swing to family rooms and the appurtenances of outdoor living. The new man-made fibers and plastics contributed to the color rampage on which America embarked in 1946. The acceptance of air conditioning and the introduction of silicone finishes brought about a revival of white in decorating. And, with Americans rated as the world's most indefatigable travelers, it is hardly surprising that the international influence, manifest in current mixtures of furniture and acces-sories, should prove to be one of the more enduring decorating trends. From all of this has emerged a dis-tinctive style, vigorous and vital, unique and indigenous, which we are proud to call Decoration U.S.A.

14

Color is acknowledged to be the most potent
and persuasive word in the decorating lexicon and yet
it has come to the fore in less than twenty years,
a rags-to-riches rise in the best American tradition.

THE COURSE OF COLOR

LIKE the course of true love, the course of color in decorating is notoriously erratic. A graph of popular preferences over the last couple of decades would show a dizzying series of peaks, plateaus and plunges as one color rose in esteem while others fell or leveled off. The response to color is more emotional than rational, and we quickly become bored with one color scheme and switch allegiance to another, partly because the color-conscious eye seeks relief or fresh stimulus, but mainly because as a nation of consumers we have had a long conditioning to sudden, radical color changes. The American love affair with color began in 1946 as an inevitable reaction against wartime drabness. The vociferous demand for home furnishings in shades other than Dubonnet red, taupe and battleship gray, voiced through a poll conducted in *House & Garden* magazine, had to some extent been anticipated by interior designers, although it caught most manufacturers unawares. Faced with a dearth of European imports, these designers had fabrics made and dyed to order, and in bypassing the traditional damasks and chintzes in traditional colors that had for so long dictated decorating styles, pioneered a contemporary, completely American palette. The second breakthrough was technological. Pigmentations developed for plastics, the miracle material of the war, initiated a brighter, clearer range of colors in paint, standardized by formula, and synthetic fibers appeared in colors unknown in the natural yarns. In a few years the color revolution was established, and the initial rash of vivid but slightly crude shades had given way to gentler, subtler pastels and neutrals, in turn superseded by stronger, sharper combinations of blue and green, pink and orange. Now even wood is treated as a color. In the living room opposite, the rich tones of wood dominate the neutral background. The accents of intense pink, orange, blue and blue-green can be removed simply by changing the sofa cushion covers, but the wood fireplace facing and ceiling canopy will remain to sponsor another color scheme.

IN THE YEARS after 1946, decorating followed a series of trends or "Looks," many pegged to a color or combination of colors. One of the more widely copied was an updated version of the White Look, a luxury previously reserved for those rich enough to afford an all-white room for appearance's sake alone. As the original White Look had been launched in London by decorator Syrie Maugham (known thereafter as the White Queen), and transplanted to the Hollywood of the thirties in a snowstorm of white fur rugs and draperies, it was only natural that the new cycle should originate in California, a state climatically and temperamentally sympathetic to it. The new white room opposite, more subtle in execution than its predecessors, is a mélange of white from stark to creamy, sleek to shaggy, with the cold textures of marble, paint and lacquer played off against the warmth of a long-pile rug and linen upholstery, all sparked by a small jolt of pure red.

Closely allied to the White Look but conceived in a different, more outdoor vein was the Southwest Look, above. Here the light neutrals with a yellow cast—the sand tones of the desert—were spiced with accents of hot pink, orange and mustard yellow, and teamed with the folk art of the American Indian and Mexican tin accessories (tin, a white metal, is kinder to neutrals than the yellow golds).

WHILE the White Look, thanks to the spread of air conditioning and the development of protective finishes for fabrics, achieved a certain measure of popular acclaim, it never enjoyed the widespread success of the more intense color combinations that washed across America in the fifties. Leading contenders in this pursuit of brightness were the monochromatic or one-color scheme and the adventurous mixtures of analogous colors (those next to each other in the spectrum) like blue and green, or pink and orange. The early monochromatic color schemes tended to stress light and medium values, presumably because they seemed to be safer and easier to use. It is only recently that an increasing familiarity with the properties of color has sanctioned the stronger treatment seen in the room above, where dark rich tones of blue are teamed with wood, lightened only by white and an enlivening touch of hot pink. Although a glance through the window would have been sufficient to

establish that nature had been pairing blue with green since time began, there was some initial resistance to the adoption of such a surprising—and to some, even shocking—color scheme which was eventually to prove the most enduring of all. But by the end of the fifties combinations of light pastoral blues and greens, foiled by white or by black and white, were to be seen throughout the length and breadth of the country. The blue and green color scheme is still very much with us, al-though in the room above it has taken on a different aspect. Where once the walls would have been white or pastel blue, now they are deep blue, in line with the current decorating predilection for concentrat-ing the darkest value of a color on the largest area of a room. Against this background peacock blues and greens in rug and upholstery stand out sharply, tempered only by chalk and bleached white. It is clearly the infinite variations inherent in the blue and green color scheme that assure its longevity.

DESPITE the national swing to color, certain areas of the palette were originally exploited only by the more avant-garde designers. One was the range of reds. Although pink—the palest value of red—was favored in the fifties for everything from walls to wall ovens, true red was handled with circumspection. It took a period of experimentation and growing confidence before red was treated like any other color. At first it cropped up merely as an accent, often in a black-and-white color scheme. Eventually the roles were reversed, and red became dominant, black and white subsidiary, as in the room opposite, where red also coexists with wood tones, an equally unexpected innovation. Now we have rooms with red walls, rooms with red upholstery, all-red rooms, with white to cool their fiery splendor. A dramatic but rare use of red appears in the bedroom below, where red is pitted against another primary color, blue, of equal intensity. This is one of the hardest color schemes to control, and its success here is due mainly to a profusion of white, the buffer between two powerful colors, and the print of bedspread and hangings, in which red and blue are mingled with softer complementary shades of purple and green, all crisply and sharply detailed against a field of white.

IS COLOR COMING TO THE END OF THE RAINBOW?

FOLLOWING in the wake of the neutrals and pastels, monochromatic schemes and two-color combinations came the Multicolor Look, probably the most ambitious of all the experiments and innovations. As this called for an adroit balance between colors of equal intensity it proved to be one of the more difficult decorating schemes to carry out, requiring a high degree of daring and discrimination, and for this reason never achieved the ready acceptance of the more straightforward color schemes. Exponents of the Multicolor Look found it easiest to start with one major element (a printed fabric or wallpaper, a large rug or painting), in which all the colors were combined, and then to distribute them judiciously throughout the room, some as accents, others over large areas. In the living room opposite, the flower-printed slip covers concentrate the main color and pattern in the center of the floor, where the brilliance can be mitigated by an off-white rug. From here the dominant red and yellow tones are dispersed around the room, but in reversed proportions. Red, the background of the print, is confined to the draperies, while yellow, no more than a minor note in the slip-cover fabric, is lavished over the walls and picked up in the cover of a third armchair. Not all versions of the Multicolor Look were as vibrant and arresting as this. Many were combinations of soft pastel pinks, blues, greens and yellows mingled with white, but even in these paler interpretations the same principles of balance applied.

Although a comparatively short-lived phenomenon, the Multicolor Look started a trend toward rich, true colors such as the stained-glass shades of red and purple, the intense high-key tones of Bristol blue and Empire green rather than the more naturalistic palette of the past, a trend that has prevailed for the past decade. At this point, when it seems the color cycle has run through every possible permutation, even the most experienced poll taker would find it impossible to predict what will come next. Without doubt, color is solidly established in America as a way of life, for, whereas it was initially confined to the conventional fields of fabrics and wallpapers, rugs and paint, now there is almost nothing you can name that does not come in color, a word that every manufacturer has found will sway sales in his favor. Plywood can be bought prefinished in colors, stained woods may be painted over without initial stripping—a fact that has spurred the vogue for painted furniture. Even the old-time practice of stenciling has been revived in brand-new contemporary versions for floors, walls and furniture.

At this moment the American household is probably the most colorful in the world, Latin America and Southeast Asia notwithstanding. Whether this will continue remains to be seen. Already there have been signs that our appetite for color has become sated and our taste is following a new bent. In many present-day rooms, color is contained in art and accessories, while the background is so restrained as to be almost unnoticeable. The current decorating fashion for mixing types and styles of furniture has brought an influx of the no-color contemporary materials—steel and glass, clear and opaque plastics—which make a pleasing contrast to wood tones and upholstery. In a country once starved for color, there is now such an *embarras de richesse* that we must inevitably revert, for a time at least, to a less heady and more balanced diet. With the experience of twenty years behind us, it is unlikely that we will ever again go on the all-out uninhibited color sprees of the past.

At a time when the nation's sights were set on the moon,
urban space in America was fast running out. As populations
exploded and cities had nowhere to go but up, the big squeeze
was on the four walls called home. For those who did not like this trend
but had to live with it, there was only one way out.

THE CONQUEST
OF INNER SPACE

VISUALLY impressive although it may be on the outside, much of the modern architecture-en-masse gives short shrift to the good life within. Yawning expanses of glass, a notable absence of solid walls and an abundance of floor plans that look as though they have been stamped out with a cookie cutter have somehow to be overcome, or at least offset, by decoration. And so there has arisen, phoenix-fashion, from the ashes of old outworn theories of room arrangement, a new approach, part art, part science, in which rooms are dealt with flexibly and pragmatically and space is now not so much filled as zoned for living. Some designers have gone so far as to come up with frozen furniture, as much a part of the room as the architecture. One example of this is the conversation pit opposite, a hole sunk in the floor and padded for seating that neatly answers the question of how to position the sofa without blocking the view or the window wall. The more usual way, less drastic and architectural, is to use freehand combinations of room dividers and built-ins, dual-purpose pieces and furniture placed back to back or in middle-of-the-room arrangements. This new approach, by demanding an equally dégagé style of furniture, has brought about the passing of the matched set, now almost impossible to fit into a room with any sense of style. Instead, following the current vogue for mixing furniture of varied shapes and sizes, materials and designs, manufacturers started to produce furniture lines in which the pieces went together but did not necessarily look alike—lightly scaled open-arm chairs to team with upholstered sofas, pairs of small tables, chests and benches, furniture finished on all sides so that it could be set in the center of the room. And so, while contemporary architecture has made decoration more difficult, it has put an end to the stalemate rooms of the past. The worth of wall space is more carefully calculated. Now, instead of being lined with furniture, a wall may be handed over to a large important painting, books, music or a collection—whatever will give the room an exciting new dimension.

ONE OF THE offshoots of the new approach to room arrangement is the architectural conversion of interiors that prove too inflexible for the owners' needs. Faced with the confining limits of four-square rooms, designers (many of whom are also architects) frequently rip out solid walls to enable the space to flow freely and untrammeled. This in turn encourages unconventional, out-in-the-open arrangements of furniture, art and accessories.

In the apartment shown here, one whole bedroom was destroyed in order to enlarge the living room. A curving quarter-circle wall of travertine panels now screens off the corner of the former bedroom that opened to the bathroom, making a dressing room. Although the wall does have this functional purpose, the more cogent reason for its appearance is to provide a graceful display surface for small sculptures behind the living room's conversation group (satin-finished stainless steel strips between the travertine panels are slotted to take adjustable brackets on which travertine shelves are lightly poised.) The only remaining trace of the vanished bedroom is a load-bearing column that can be glimpsed behind a sofa in the view at the right. Beyond this column is the travertine-floored foyer above, which leads to the dining

room. An absence of doors between living room and foyer, foyer and dining room, keeps the whole area open and fluid, allowing the shapes and colors of silhouetted sculpture, chrome-and-leather chairs and the paintings to stand out against pure, simple backgrounds. In the living room, the bulk of the furniture is arranged on a gray area rug in a big, three-sided conversation group that turns its back on the foyer and faces a window and a smaller seating group of sofa and upholstered armchair. Two more windows, gained when the bedroom was removed, now form an L-shaped corner (above and left), where a small round table and chairs stand ready for a game of cards, an impromptu supper or a bout of letter writing.

Another outstanding aspect of the architectural concept of room planning is the elimination of lamps from the decorating scheme. Lighting is mainly recessed in the ceiling, and where a fixture was indicated, the architect-designers had it made to their own specifications. A large suspended disk with sixteen opalescent plastic cylinders was specially designed to cast a soft, glare-free glow over the sculptured dancer, poised on a plinth, that dominates the foyer. A simple square egg-crate overhead fixture beams light on the dining table.

THE FREEDOM of furniture arrangement conferred by the flowing space of the open plan now extends to even those older apartments traditionally split up into a series of separate rooms. All that is required is the courage to take down walls and the realism to keep furniture in check. In this apartment, the foyer, living room and dining room

were thrown together to make the one big open area below, with only a partial divider wall remaining to give privacy to the dining table and chairs and firm backing to the spinet. The seating group, marked off from the white-tiled foyer and dining area by wall-to-wall carpeting, has little furniture —a sofa, two armchairs, a coffee table and Eames lounge chair—but all of it is large enough in scale to take the place of a huddle of smaller pieces. Built-ins along the fireplace wall house books and a music system. Apart from a lone table lamp, lighting consists of spotlights fastened to wood strips between the ceiling beams and painted a matching white to blend into the background.

WHEN WALLS become windows, furniture must perforce move elsewhere. The tendency today is to go to the other extreme and put the bulk of the furniture—the inescapable conversation group—smack in the middle of the room, in some cases marking off the limits with an area rug and frequently backing the sofa with a long low table, desk or chests of equal height. This kind of arrangement, by creating a room within a room, gives the seating group more authority than if it were simply cast adrift in the center of the floor. In an open-plan living room it also answers the question of where to put the dining or other storage units when all the wall space has been taken up. However, the pairing of a straight-lined sofa and chests calls for small pull-up pieces to give the group flexibility and chairs with curving contours to offset the prevailing long horizontal lines. As a middle-of-the-room seating arrangement usually turns its back on —or at least away from—the view, there should always be some strong, sizable focal point toward which the sofa can be oriented. This can be as simple as the wall assemblage of TV, music and paintings in the apartment above, or as striking as the art-hung wood fireplace wall and cantilevered hearth in the glass-walled living room opposite. Or it might be a mural, a beautifully displayed collection, a Coromandel screen or an antique armoire.

AT THE pinnacle of city living stands the penthouse apartment, urban equivalent of the glass-walled house. The raison d'être of a penthouse is the view, and in this apartment, where dividing walls between foyer, living room and dining room had been removed to let in light and the river scene, the resulting size and stature of the room presented a problem of arrangement. Huge rooms are notoriously harder to handle than the less grand, for small pieces of furniture tend to get swallowed up, large ones to look uneasily marooned. A surfeit of furniture can produce a room with all the less charming characteristics of an airport lounge and without the release of impending flight. In this apartment, the furniture, over-scaled but purposely scant, was skillfully anchored by blocks of bold color, which also help the room to seem more furnished than it actually is. Two islands of color mark off the living room, linked only by the neutral beige carpeting. In the main living

area, the end wall, a backdrop for books and a long white work shelf, is painted bright red. Beyond it is an out-in-the-open conversation group of two large sofas, upholstered in anemone-purple silk, two red ottomans, small occasional tables and a glass-topped coffee table centered on a blue, red and purple rya rug. Two recessed ceilings, painted deep blue, outline the seating group and the dining area at the other end of the room. Here the red wall is balanced by a buffet with red-painted doors and a powerful abstract painting. The dining furniture, however, is in direct contrast to the brilliance of the conversation group, for an equally intense color scheme would have given the room a seesaw effect, each half competing with the other. Instead, the table is white marble with a silvery metal frame, the chairs simple slings of natural leather on metal. The final block of color, a blue-painted free-standing panel, displays stone sculptures and screens the dining area from the foyer.

WITH SPACE shrinking and rents rising, the one-room apartment is now not so much a temporary pied-à-terre as a permanent way of life. That it can be a civilized, even elegant way of life is amply demonstrated by this apartment, where the confines of one large room (plus kitchen and bathroom) are treated in such a way as to be not in the least confining. Although the everyday necessities of eating and sleeping are incorporated, they are not allowed to interfere with the over-all appearance of the apartment, designed to look well from any angle, at any time. Doors in a storage and book wall at one end of the living area, below, open to disclose a Murphy bed, but not the hole-in-the-wall eyesore of the past. This bed boasts an alcove lined with blue felt, a Tamayo painting and French Empire bust on a display shelf. Similarly, the dining group, a marble-topped table and bent-

wood chairs, is also set off by a painting and shelf arrangement of candlesticks and objects.

In the part of the room allocated to seating, sleep and study (a large desk is set conveniently near reference books in the storage wall), sofas, chairs and tables are spread out around a large white area rug in a flexible furniture arrangement that can be tightened into one large circle or split into smaller groups. Although all the furniture in the apartment is of the contemporary off-the-floor type that keeps space open and uncrowded, there is great variety in the materials, shapes and colors: a bright-blue sofa, Bertoia chairs upholstered in burnt orange fabric, a black leather Eames chair, Barcelona chairs in natural leather and contemporary versions of nineteenth-century bentwood. A profusion of plants, paintings and sculpture set against plain walls, white curtains and translucent plastic panels and picked out by pole lights helps the apartment to achieve a sophistication that belies its size.

Zoning, a commonplace in city-planning terminology, has worked its way into the decorating lexicon as a synonym for the adroit interior planning that splits one room into many parts, each with a different and definite purpose. In this small one-room apartment the zoning is so skillful as to be imperceptible. At first glance this appears to be a well-furnished living room. Only closer examination reveals that it is actually a series of interlocking groups for seating and sleeping, eating and entertaining, study and relaxation. A tiny foyer, papered and curtained with a dimensional green-and-white cane print, leads to a small seating group (shown left and below) where a sofa that opens to put up a guest, two armless chairs and a bamboo corner chair cluster around a coffee table and needlepoint accent rug. At the opposite end of the room a big shaggy sheepskin rug draws at-

tention to the main fireplace group of a day bed and chaise at the right, both covered in green-and-white toile, a pair of cane-backed fauteuils and a long lacquered table that is both desk and dining table. Bridging the two groups, a second table identical in shape and color but lower in height is set in front of the window wall, below, to serve as a buffet for parties, a display surface at other times. Space-stretching ideas make the room seem larger than it is. The color scheme is airy and light. Instead of fussy curtaining, the windows are screened by white vertical louvered blinds. Furniture with open lines is concentrated near the windows; more solid, light-blocking pieces are kept to the walls. Mirrored alcoves flanking the fireplace as backing for books and paintings give an illusory depth, while the wall above the mantel is kept purposely unornamented and therefore unobtrusive.

As the typical modern apartment is apt to be functional but featureless, it is left to the designer to build character where none exists. Such architectural additions as stock moldings applied to plain walls at ceiling and chair-rail height, rush screens and paneling and a built-in bookcase did a great deal to improve the appearance of the apartment below, but only adroit furniture arrange-

ment could make it comfortable and livable. Contrary to the less-is-more concept of space planning, where furniture is kept to the essential minimum, this apartment has an unusual number of chairs, sofas and tables. Yet, although it is agreeably cluttered (clutter, well controlled, is coming back into fashion), it is in no way crowded. The dining room below, left—rated as a room because it

is closed off from the living area by fixed and folding screens but actually no more than a dining area—holds a table and four French Directoire chairs which can be moved into the living room to supplement seating. The living room itself is neatly divided by Moroccan area rugs in reverse colors— one dark, one light, each forming the nucleus of a seating group. The larger of the groups, in front of French windows leading to a terrace, easily accommodates twin Spanish love seats bridged by a pair of Louis XV chairs and a coffee table. In the smaller group, spaced out to leave the floor free in the center of the room, a table, leather bergère and open-arm chair (akin to those in the dining room) cluster by one wall, a Louis XV desk and chair are at right angles to the wall opposite.

After years of plain painted walls plus solid-color carpeting
and curtains, the decoration of walls, floors and windows is running riot
with pattern piled on pattern, texture teamed with texture,
shape set against shape. Backgrounds are back in business
and it all adds up to an exciting new status for the shell we inhabit.

THE BOLD BACKGROUND

ONE OF the most welcome sights of the past decade has been the re-emergence of walls, floors and windows from decorating obscurity. At one point it seemed that backgrounds were about to fade away completely. Color schemes were pallid, architecture promoted the smooth, sleek plane, and a good part of the country was sold on shibui (fine in its place, but a strange negation of the dominant principles of Western decoration). Apart from a few determined spirits who clung to their rose-covered bedrooms and Oriental rugs, and a covey of far-sighted designers who recognized the timeless power of pattern, the prevailing decorative mood was one of simplicity bordering on starkness. Anyone with a desire for a different kind of background was out of luck, for the choices were few and uninspiring. Wallpaper stuck to traditional colors and patterns, carpeting was mostly wall-to-wall broadloom in a limited range of shades, and curtain fabrics were either coyly patterned or uncompromisingly plain. As in the case of color, the response to the inevitable public reaction against such limitations came swiftly. Wallpaper companies ventured into contemporary colors and patterns, co-ordinated papers and fabrics took over walls and windows, and manufacturers of hard-surface floorings, capitalizing on the chameleon properties of vinyl, began to copy real textures, such as parquet, flagstone, cork and marble. Today, it is hard to remember how recently most of these innovations came about. Yet, who, twenty or even ten years ago, would have dared to put three strong patterns in a room like the one opposite? The combination of blue-and-white striped ticking, leopard-print upholstery and an octagonal ceramic tile floor might then quite rightly have been considered expensive insanity. The upholstery would undoubtedly have been real instead of fake fur, and the ticking on the walls would have been there to stay—whereas now it comes paper-backed and can be removed at will. This is the main reason why pattern is back in backgrounds. It is strictly expendable and can easily be turned in for something new the minute it palls.

A more permanent part of the picture is the architectural background, so called because it is built right into the house itself. In the living room opposite, this was accomplished by simply continuing exterior stone and batten walls, though if the purpose had merely been to embellish plain plaster walls in a less costly manner, the wood could have been laminated paneling and the stone a composition or vinyl facsimile. Where once this kind of background would have automatically implied a rustic interior of the hunting-lodge type, now it is chic to ignore the obvious in favor of abstract oils, silk-upholstered sofas and chairs and Oriental ex-otica. Contrast is all, and the bolder the contrast, the better the room.

Nowadays a plain wall is a positive invitation to be dashing or daring—provided, of course, that the room (and the owner) can take it. Something as unusual as the mock medieval tapestry below (painted on canvas and then attached to the walls) is rightly reserved for rooms that are fairly small, underfurnished and intended only for part-time pursuits like playing cards or paying bills. Then it is also permissible to throw in, completely out of context and sheerly for its singularly delightful shape, a hooded hallporter's chair.

As the vogue for texture in backgrounds took hold, brick—a humble material that had been around since the Pharaohs—came into its own. To the amazement of contractors (a rather hidebound breed), many people started to insist on leaving brick in its natural state rather than slicking it over with plaster or, in old houses, stripping the wall down to the bone and letting the brick show through. Old bricks, considered superior in texture, color and patina to the new, were hunted like uranium and the sites of wrecked buildings raided at dead of night. As a background, brick proved surprisingly adaptable. To find a brick wall and polished herringbone-pattern brick floor in the modern Southwestern glass-walled house opposite is not too unexpected. The timeless quality of brick is obviously intended to marry the architecture to an eclectic collection of furniture, ranging from an early Mission table and seventeenth-century Savonarola chair to a nineteenth-century bentwood rocker and a giddily carved and gilded chest from present-day Mexico. It does, however, come as a slight shock to see how well brick communes with a reproduction Tudor armoire, eighteenth-century open-arm chairs, table full-skirted in the Victorian manner and modern zebra-skin rugs in the much more sophisticated setting above. But notice the small, subtle touch that takes away the rough, unfinished look of the brick: a frieze of wooden zodiac plaques, artfully arranged to top the wall with a smooth decorative band of contrasting texture in the style of the eighteenth century.

Not only natural textures but also the patterned papers and fabrics used long ago to give an illusion of warmth and intimacy to the echoing rooms of stately mansions came back into fashion as the decorative background was re-established. The old damask wallpapers were revived and updated. Printed in bold black and white rather than the traditional colors, and teamed with a deep red rug and an overscaled black-and-white hound's-tooth upholstery fabric, the damask wallpaper in the room at the right acquires a new contemporary character without sacrificing the intrinsic elegance of the design. The fabric-covered wall—a necessary stratagem in centuries when steam heat was nonexistent—turned out to have as much merit for cliff dwellers as for château owners. The tapestry-like qualities of a richly patterned fabric could be counted on to make a small and hitherto undistinguished foyer like the one below seem both furnished and inviting while the insulating qualities of the fabric—especially if reinforced by urethane

48

foam—proved to be one of the less costly ways to shut out sounds from the next-door apartment.

Another auspicious aspect of the fabric-covered wall that had been overlooked for years and now swept back into style was its effectiveness as a background for art and accessories. Provided that the colors were muted and the design regular and decisive, unrelated objects and paintings were actually given unity by a patterned wall—witness the grouping above, a rather oddly assorted collection disciplined by the small-scale all-over print and vertical stripe of the fabric. Yet, despite its many manifest advantages, fabric might not have been so wholeheartedly adopted without the proofing processes that made its surface resistant to dirt, stains and moisture, and also the advances in installation techniques. Notoriously hard to hang, fabric foiled most amateur attempts until the advent of better adhesives, Velcro tape (a self-locking nylon strip that glues or stitches to plaster, wood and fabric) and the paper-backed fabrics. From then on, even such mutinous materials as linen, burlap, ticking and felt could be, and were, hung wholesale.

Rivaling in popularity the well-established papers and fabrics, all kinds of coverings—real, fake and photographically reproduced—began to spread over the nation's walls. The initial vogue for such natural textures as grasscloth, wood veneers and brick, cork and bamboo became gradually overshadowed by the spectacular rise of the unnaturals, products of the plastic age that followed the venerable trompe l'œil tradition in aping their betters. Screen-printed vinyl was especially successful in simulating the real thing in a way that the Venetians, past masters of decorative deception with paint, might have envied. In the foyer above left, what appears at first to be fragile silk wallpaper with a delicate tracery of bamboo is actually vinyl.

Another popular device for breaking the monotony of the bare background—artificial architecture—re-created in paper the craftsmanship of the past. Paper panels and moldings imitated the beautiful boiserie and superb plasterwork found in the great

eighteenth-century houses of England and France, marbleized paper emulated the commanding columns of Italy. Stock architectural moldings were combined with paper or vinyl to give the impression of a dado, and period paneling was reproduced by the simple expedient of pasting rectangles of an appropriate paper or fabric onto the wall and then framing the panels with half rounds, an easy and inexpensive wall treatment which, teamed with a low chest and a pair of chairs in the small dining room above right, takes the place of a large, imposing piece of furniture. A further extension of the architectural effect was the three-dimensional composition wall block made to resemble natural brick or sculptured stone. These blocks, although light enough to be glued in place, looked uncannily true to life, giving them a distinct edge over the flat-faced paper architecture. In the guest room opposite, a demi-wall of make-believe stone pits pattern and texture against a plain flat painted wall.

PATTERN HOLDS THE FLOOR
IN THE BOLD BACKGROUND

THERE is no quicker way to direct attention to one particular part of a room than to cover it with pattern. Floors, like walls, were long the stepchildren of decoration, seldom shown off with pride, mostly muffled in yards of drab solid-color carpeting about as provocative as a uniform. Unlike walls, floors had to wait for a considerable time before being taken over by pattern. Conversion of looms to contemporary designs and colors represented more capital outlay than a switch to a different kind of wallpaper design. The carpet companies bided their time, waiting until the trend to bolder colors and patterns was definitely established and proved to be no passing fancy. In fact, it is only within the last ten years that American rug companies have brought out so many new colors, patterns, materials, sizes and shapes that the results are clearly apparent on every level of taste and price. First to be seriously affected by the postwar wind of change was that firmly rooted standby without which, at one time, no house was considered well furnished—wall-to-wall carpeting. Where a family could once count on settling into a house and moving no more than once or twice, if at all, now the tenure, especially of families at the junior-executive level, was short-lived.

With mobility an inescapable fact of American life, the amount of cutting and stitching required to make last year's wall-to-wall carpet (a considerable cash investment) fit into this year's living room became a major decorating headache. The result was inevitable: wall-to-wall carpeting gave way to the easier-to-place room-size or area rug. Apart from its practicality, the smaller rug had other points in its favor. In strictly contemporary rooms where the architecture was nondescript and the furniture relatively straight-lined and simple, a richly patterned or deeply carved rug brought the decoration down to earth, focusing interest on the floor or helping to define a scattered furniture grouping. Such is the case in the room opposite, where two area rugs, similar in pattern and color, although slightly different in size, neatly separate the room into two parts, one for dining, one for sitting, without blocking or compartmenting the floor space. The low ceiling, a bugbear of present-day apartments, is offset by the striking borders, which direct the eye down rather than up. Not so obvious but equally important is the fact that area rugs like this can not only be turned to equalize wear and tear but also replaced in summer by a rug of a different persuasion—straw or sisal, cotton or nylon—or even, in this age of prefinished, easy-to-clean wood floors, no rug at all, thus changing the whole mood of the room in a mattter of minutes. As rugs diminished in size (the accent rug, small but puissant in design, was often the only soft touch on a hard floor), pattern and color became increasingly important. Instead of the muted, nondescript shades of the past, carpeting emerged in strong and vibrant tones of nasturtium and purple, raspberry red and Bristol blue, aided by the new synthetic fibers that, being colorless themselves, could be dyed the most brilliant colors. Such exotic imports as the Scandinavian rya rugs, long in pile and blurrily beautiful as an abstract painting (some owners, reluctant to tread on them, actually hung these rugs on their walls), the gaily colored and tasseled Spanish bedspreads which were used as rugs, and a flock of other candidates from all over the world soon revived the honorable and venerable tradition of the patterned rug.

An offshoot of this was the overdue revival of the Oriental rug, long out of fashion. Oriental rugs laid on bare polished floors, instead of overlaid on carpeting as formerly, were newly recognized as things of beauty. Soon Oriental rugs languishing in warehouses assumed the status of collectors' items (a few were, many more were not), which only goes to show that if you hold on to something long enough, it is bound to come back into style.

With all the best floors sporting pattern, it was inevitable that even conservative halls and stairways would relinquish solid-color carpeting in favor of something as daring as spotted leopard (teamed at the right in the true pattern-on-pattern spirit with a damask wallpaper and a striped Roman shade). The prevalence of strong pattern and color in rugs soon made it perfectly plausible and relatively simple to build a color scheme from the ground up. The patterned rug in the room opposite, a striking alternation of high and low pile, shaggy and smooth textures achieved through an intricate fusion of hand work and machine craft, has all the dominance of a true work of art. The flamboyance of the colors and the scale of the pattern, unusual in a rug as large as this, are deliberately calculated to initiate in a neutral room a dramatic, vibrant color scheme, repeated in small accents, in much the same way that an enormous abstract painting might be used. It takes a rug of such authority to stand out in this vast room against overscaled furniture; anything weaker in design or softer in color would tend to fade out.

Perhaps one of the most important characteristics of the patterned rug in decorating is this ability to impose order, form and effect. For instance, a simple striped rug can visually widen or lengthen a room. A round, patterned rug, in addition to determining the configuration of a conversation or dining group (which a plain rug can do perfectly

adequately) also gives the chairs and tables a more interesting and compelling background. Where the furniture is sparse and not particularly distinguished, a superb Chinese or Oriental rug can be a saving grace. Fur rugs, qualified as patterned by the subtlety of their shadings, are luxurious enough to make the barest living room or bedroom seem lavishly furnished. As the field of pattern in rugs encompasses everything from the traditional woven designs to the wilder shores of hand-crafted abstraction, it is an easy matter to find something to suit any period or style of decoration.

The perennially popular needle-point rug, now made in less expensive machine versions and contemporary colors, can act as a bridge between modern and traditional furnishings, like the needle-point carpet of flowers in the country living room at the left. For a room like the one below, where the furniture is clean-lined and contemporary, the disciplined geometrics of a Moroccan rug add needed color and pattern without being overpowering. The rug in the room opposite has a stylized design and timeless quality completely in accord with the variety of furnishings: contemporary chairs, sofa and coffee table, an oak console table carved in the seventeenth-century manner and velvet-covered camp stools that derive from the Greco-Roman curule.

THE HARD FACTS OF PRESENT-DAY FLOORS

ONE OF THE more ubiquitous discoveries of this generation is undoubtedly vinyl tile, the hard-surfaced flooring that changes its face to suit the company it keeps. Parquet, marble, terrazzo, brick, ceramic tile and flagstone are but a few of the ancestors that vinyl can claim and simulate, although it has yet to advance one step further and set an intrinsic style of its own, non-imitative and true to the nature and characteristics of the material. However, considering the relatively short space of time vinyl has been with us it may be unfair to expect such a radical development before all the familiar routines have been exhausted. Effortlessly supplanting the immediate predecessors in the field of hard flooring—asphalt tile and rubber tile—vinyl first came to the surface with the checkerboard black-and-white tile floor, a vinyl equivalent of the classic marble pattern that became a decorating cliché, albeit an excellent one. (A widely published photograph of that particular vinyl floor, combined with accents of strong orange, probably did more than anything to launch the black and white plus color trend.) Vinyl has come a long way since then, and, although there have been occasional excesses committed in its name—notably the insertion of metallic flecks and other extraneous matter—the results have been praiseworthy. Nothing is as versatile as vinyl. Teamed with Biedermeier furniture, below left, textured vinyl is laid in a pattern resembling an Empire wood parquet floor. In the living room opposite, the tiles pursue the rambling outlines of flagstone, while the open-plan living and dining room, below right, benefits from wood-grain vinyl arranged in a simple herringbone design that helps to unify the mixture of furniture.

Undoubtedly, the greatest advantage of vinyl as a decorative floor covering is its amazing ability to reproduce different textures and designs, capturing the quintessence of a classic material in a practical contemporary form. In the dining room opposite, blue, green and white vinyl tile are cleverly combined to suggest the three-dimensional look of the intricate intarsia marble floors seen in Florentine palaces, thus giving a regal ambience to a rather sparsely furnished room. Another example is the dining room, above right. Here another classic copied in vinyl, Delft tile, not only paves the floor but continues on and up to form a dado and wall panel in a modern version of an old Dutch interior. In both cases, the flooring establishes and carries through the decorative theme, allowing a fair amount of latitude in the choice of furnishings.

A comparatively recent development in the short but spectacular history of vinyl tile is the introduction of laminates. Actual materials, from wood

veneers and cane to pebbles and mother-of-pearl are encased in clear vinyl, resulting in a hard sleek surface with the original texture literally frozen underneath. In the study, above left, the inescapable fake leopard has been trapped in a vinyl cage and then laid in squares divided by strips of wood-grain vinyl, an amusing conceit for a small bathroom or foyer. Although this incorporation of one material in another is not new in principle (terrazzo, a traditional flooring, is merely a mixture of marble chips and concrete, highly polished), the innovation lies in the lamination of materials. The prospect of tiles in which the patterns underfoot will not be imitations but as authentic as a picture under glass, and the techniques that give man-made rugs all the subtlety and variety of design, pile and color gradation once achieved only by handcraftsmanship have opened up a new world of beauty for floor coverings. The future is limited only by the designers' imagination.

WINDOW DRESSING LOOMS LARGE
IN THE BOLD BACKGROUND

DESPITE the inroads of contemporary architecture, walls and floors have managed to cling to their basic contours, and the curved wall or raked floor are seldom seen outside avant-garde museums. Not so with windows, which have been steadily modified ever since the introduction of the sliding panels and walls of glass common to most modern houses. The clerestory window, the peaked two-story window that accompanies a cathedral living room or an A-frame, and the window that turns a corner are some of the more conspicuous divergences in design that have taken the place of the old double-hung or casement windows.

The decorative treatment of windows has passed through an equal number of phases. According to the mood and manner of the times, windows have been covered in every conceivable fashion. First they were muffled with heavy draperies or demurely hidden by café curtains and ruffled tiebacks. With the advent of ready-made, drip-dry sheers they appeared daringly sheathed in yards of revealing, light-filtering fabric. The beguiling shirred Austrian curtain enjoyed a brief and heady popularity (over-exposure caused its demise) until superseded by the trimmer Roman shade. Then came the so-called architectural treatment, in which panels of paper, plastic or fabric were hung on tracks or arranged as screens in front of the windows—a trend directly traceable to the influence of shoji, adopted wholesale in the fifties when the prestige of Japanese design was at its height. Another type of architectural window screening was the pierced panels or louvered shutters of wood that completely masked the glass and yet let in enough light. Commerce contributed new ideas such as vertical plastic louvers, a sidewise adapta-

tion of the Venetian blind principle used to control light on the immense all-glass façades of modern buildings. Within the last few years there has been an upsurge of window shades—not the old-fashioned green, dark blue or white roller shade that did little more than live up to its name, but contemporary versions as decoratively giddy as the hand-painted "paper curtains" of the Directoire and Victorian eras. Infinitely more practical than their predecessors, these updated shades are laminated or vinyl-impregnated, washable, made of both paper and fabric and painted, screen-printed or dyed in a far-reaching range of colors. Although many of the shades are pretty enough to hang alone, they are often combined with floor-length draperies, a hard-against-soft contrast that, like a patterned rug on a plain floor, gives the window greater dimension and interest.

A versatile team of sheer curtains and shades is shown in the city living room opposite. Each window is fitted with two shades—one permanent overshade and one undershade that can be changed according to a seasonal switch in color scheme. In the top, cold-weather version, a rich raspberry red shade pulls down behind its printed companion to match the red-lacquered bentwood chairs, red area rug and sofa pillows. For the second, summer color scheme of neutral and gold tones, gold-and-white printed shades replace the cold-weather shades, ottomans upholstered in the same fabric as the sofa take the place of the bentwood chairs, the rug and pillows are changed and panels of yellow burlap hung on either side of the fireplace. With minor replacements of accessories, the room is ready for a different season. Apart from the purely decorative aspect, the underlying purpose

of this and most previous window treatments is to tame the light of day and ensure some measure of privacy at night. Window walls with their wealth of glass are naturally the most demanding, and the problem is compounded when the windows are not fixed, but sliding panels opening outdoors.

In an inspired deviation from conventional methods of curtaining, the floor-to-ceiling sliding window wall in the room opposite is screened not on the inside but on the outside with canvas tie-back draperies, hung from a sliding track, that match the canvas awning. This neat solution has the added merit of cutting glare and heat by shielding the glass from the direct rays of the sun. Another form of screening with curtains is practiced in the traditional living room above, where the major problem was a radiator that protruded below the window sill—common to old houses where radiators and air conditioners are not built in. Here three different kinds of window covering are neatly combined: matchstick bamboo blinds to screen the window and diffuse the light, printed café curtains hung from a pole at sill height to disguise the radiator, and solid-color tie-back draperies, lined with the same printed cotton used for the café curtains, to soften the outlines of the window.

Where a window wall does not exist—and the desire for one does—a wall with only one or two small windows is often strategically screened to give the impression that behind lies an expanse of glass. Instead of being curtained, the two windows on the end wall of the living room below are covered

against which the shapes of accessories on top of the built-in bookshelves stand out in sharp relief.

A totally different but equally striking use of screens in the dining area opposite compensates for both the paucity of windows (there is only one in the center of the wall) and an architectural double

by a series of sliding linen panels, weighted by rods at the bottom and hung from a double ceiling track that enables them to overlap or to be pulled back independently to let in daylight. In colors ranging from beige through yellow to orange and red, the panels constitute a brilliant backdrop

jog at the sides. The window is curtained with floor-length sheer draperies and the sides camouflaged by free-standing wood screens, the centers of which have been cut out in the style of a Gothic arch and then filled in with the same open-weave fabric that hangs at the entrance to the dining area.

One of the more celebrated of all the architectural window coverings is the pierced panel or grillework screen, which is to glass what a veil is to a woman—both mask and lure. The grille, originating in Moorish and Oriental architecture, is by no means new. Common for centuries throughout the Middle East and Spain, it cropped up again in Lima's Churrigueresque, enclosed, carved wood balconies. Until fairly recently, the grille had been confined to countries with a history of secrecy or seclusion, where custom required that the occupants of a house might look out but no one could look in. Why, then, should twentieth-century Americans, whose lives were presumably an open book, so wholeheartedly adopt such an enigmatic and antisocial element? The grille's sudden and surprising popularity can be directly linked to a fashion of the fifties set by one of America's leading and most widely copied architects, Edward Durell Stone. Disposed before, behind and around his public buildings and private houses, the grille became his trademark and a status symbol for the whole country. As this coincided with a time when many people were growing painfully conscious of being overobserved, the grille, with its close relations—fretwork, trelliswork and latticework—was soon a decorative institution.

Grilles of plaster or similarly immobile materials were usually fixed, while those of metal or wood could be hinged or fitted into tracks. The bay window opposite, covered by two fixed side panels and four sliding center panels, allows a compromise. The view can be completely screened off, with only sunlight filtering through the openwork panels, or, on a particularly spectacular day, it may be completely revealed. For large windows like this or for window walls, grilles are a neater solution than yards of fussy fabric which make a room seem closed in and as a long-term investment they frequently prove to be far less expensive.

Although it has been generally agreed that living in close touch with nature is one of the benefits bestowed on humanity by modern architecture and insulated glass, living in the full glare of nature's spotlight is not. To restrain the powerful light that pours through high and wide windows, every conceivable device has been called on, including some so familiar or venerable that they were almost overlooked. One example is the Venetian blind, the rage of the eighteenth century, now regarded as something the landlord provides until the curtains come. In the bedroom below left, an expanse of glass wall divided into sections by false beams is covered by a row of brilliantly colored Venetian blinds that fit neatly between the divisions. (Color, achieved through paint or the lamination of fabric to the slats, and the disappearance of dangling cords and ropes, are two valid reasons why the Venetian blind is again allowed to show its face, instead of being covered with a curtain.) Shoji, the standby of the Japanese (whose houses, although smaller, are equally exposed) are no longer for the few but for the mass market. Be that as it may, shoji still represent one of the easiest, quickest and least expensive ways to cover up a window wall, because both they and the windows come in stock sizes. Hinged to the wall, as they are in the boy's bedroom below right, they can be folded back in the daytime. Then there is the roller shade, second only to the Venetian blind in length of tenure. Roller shades are about the only covering you can hang over a sliding door that will get out of the way fast when the door has to be opened. They are also fashioned in special shapes to fit into special spots such as the odd-shaped windows at the top of the window wall opposite. (Other versions, designed for skylights, roll sideways.) That old truism about there being nothing new under the sun certainly bears remembering so far as window treatments are concerned.

Two direct results of the sweeping social changes in postwar America
were the almost total disappearance of domestic help and the decline
of the large family house. As the rooms on the blueprint
were re-evaluated in terms of self-service and space saving, most of them
emerged changed beyond all recognition—and all the better for it.

ROOMS THAT SAY U.S.A.

SET AN American house down anywhere in the world and it will clearly and unmistakably proclaim its origin. Yet the typical American house as we know it today is a comparatively recent phenomenon. Before 1941, most families were comfortably ensconced in the same kind of home that had survived in essence for a century or more, where every room had an acknowledged role and was devoted exclusively to sitting, cooking, eating, sleeping or, if the house was large enough, to playing the piano, reading or studying. Only the parlor, relic of a Victorian convention of polite conversation in acute discomfort, had really gone out of style, although many of the remaining rooms were almost as seldom used and just about as outmoded. After 1945 all this was changed. The irreplaceable domestic servant vanished into industry and emerged on the far side of housework. A postwar population explosion brought a rash of new housing, mostly compact structures cut to a minimal pattern that would reduce costs of labor and materials. Space was redesigned to give greater efficiency in smaller quarters. Rooms were telescoped, and the words open plan and dual purpose became a part of the language. Dining, a part-time activity, was relegated (as opposite) to any odd corner of the living room that would accommodate a table and chairs. Music and books, which had once rated rooms of their own, were now lucky to be squeezed into one end of an open-plan living room or, later, the family room, while any more cerebral ventures had perforce to be pursued in the privacy of the bedroom. This state of affairs, summed up in the once-prevalent phrase "togetherness," ran its course with an undercurrent of frayed nerves and lapsed manners, the usual concomitants of enforced communal living. In the process, trying though it must have been to the pioneers, a new and totally American concept of a house emerged, in which the allocation of interior space was no longer dictated by custom but considered empirically. It is this concept we follow today in the planning of rooms, without regard to what was once the determining factor—the size of the house.

Room for dining, in this context, does not necessarily mean an out-and-out dining room. Many people prefer, as much for reasons of expediency as space, to bring dining into the living room, thus making the transition from cocktails to dinner a simple matter of moving over. For those who appreciate a sense of separation, the dining platform offers an admirable compromise. Two steps higher than the living room and semiscreened, the dining platform above seems like another room,

although the similarity of color scheme and furnishings indicate that it is, in fact, an offshoot of the living room. Another dining platform above also follows the color scheme set by the lower level but reverses the proportions. Pumpkin, used as an accent color on sofa cushions, takes over the tile floor of the dining platform and the seats of the dining chairs. As this dining platform is a dominant part of the room, it was made more attractive by adding an indoor pool, plants and chandeliers.

The part of a living room given over to dining does not always conform to the prevailing decoration. It can, in fact, be much more effective if totally unanticipated. Tucked in the bay-window recess of a large living room, the dining area above is distinguished by the remarkable, overscaled antique dining furniture—seventeenth-century chairs with caned and heavily carved backs and an immense, squat Victorian pedestal table stripped down to the natural wood—which stands out prominently against the simplicity of the background. On the other hand, it is the sheer surprise of a striped canopy, brick floor and mirrored end wall that call attention to the dining area in the center. One of the

pleasanter aspects of eating in the living room is the more comfortable form chairs have taken of late. Small-scaled open-arm chairs that can be switched from the dining table to the conversation group, even sofas and benches, are now acknowledged as acceptable. As the general height of such pieces is considerably lower than the standard dining chair, dining tables have followed suit, with the level slumping from the regular twenty-nine inches to a low of twenty-five. Although this new horizon for dining, shown above, has a long way to fall before it matches that of the Orientals or reclining Romans, it indicates a more relaxed approach to one of man's oldest pleasures—the table.

A ROOM THAT BELONGS TO EVERYONE—
THE FRIENDLY, BUSY FAMILY ROOM

THE MOST innately and distinctively American room of our generation, and certainly the most universally adopted, is the family room. Soundly based on democratic family principles, this extension and refinement of the old-time playroom or rumpus room fitted right in with the trend to informality at home that swept the country in the late forties and early fifties. As the living room had by then replaced the earlier parlor as the place supposedly reserved or at least kept ready for company, the more plebeian family room was the catchall for everything banished from view and a natural retreat for the teen-age set. Not surprisingly, the decoration was dictated less by choice than by necessity. When a room was destined to see long and hard service, it seemed hardly worthwhile to spend any time or money on it, so into it went furniture that had been honorably retired.

The salvation of the much-abused family room came with the advent of the practical, impervious plastics, vinyl floor tiles, washable wall coverings and protective finishes for furniture and fabrics. Finally, it became possible to have a room that would stand up to daily wear and tear without being refurbished every six months. As the appearance of the family room improved, its status shot up and it became the repository of the steadily increasing paraphernalia of relaxation—hi-fi and stereo systems, television, games, home movies, the bar and the barbecue fireplace (an outdoor custom that had moved indoors). No longer was the family room just a place for the family to gather; it was also the place where the family entertained. Guests were more apt to be taken into the family room (where the latest acquisition would be pointed to with pride) than into the living room, which,

paradoxically, forthwith turned into a less self-conscious and much more comfortable part of the house. Since the family room had, in effect, evolved into a second, breezier living room, the makeshifts that had once been tolerated were no longer acceptable. Strictly utilitarian interiors were abandoned in favor of sophistication and style. Although decoration for the most part was in the contemporary vein, it was not considered at all out of keeping for a family room to be furnished in French Provincial reproductions.

A perfect example of the latter-day family room is shown opposite. Impressive without being oppressive, it is designed to live up to any family event, from a small adult party around the fireplace to a full-scale dance on the ceramic tile floor. At first glance, the room seems almost bare, but it is amply furnished with a huge sofa, ottomans and an off-in-the-corner game group. A breath of the outdoors, customary in many houses that have to exist in an air-conditioned climate (this house is in Texas) is introduced by plants set in brick troughs around the edge of the floor. Although such a special room was obviously part of the integral design of the house, families not so favored are seldom deterred by the apparent lack of opportune space. Attics and basements of older houses are converted, and sun porches or verandas glassed in and heated. In cramped new houses, the garage is often pre-empted for the family room. Where a house is designed on the open-plan principle, a family room is frequently incorporated with the kitchen. The ultimate family room is sometimes situated in a separate structure, such as a pool house, and doubles as guest suite, which is about as far up the ladder as a family room can go.

Just as the decoration of a family room varies according to climate, environment and social standing, in addition to the tastes of the owners and the number and ages of their children, so perhaps the only thing all family rooms have in common is their ability to take abuse gracefully. Surfaces are apt to be more rugged than in the living room, furnishings easy to maintain. Wood and plastic, wrought iron and inexpensive washable cotton are

the mainstays of this family room, a converted sun porch at the back of a traditional house. There are no rugs, only a bare polished wood floor—an indication that dancing ranks high in the interests of the younger generation—and the walls are plain random planking. Because the long narrow confines of the old porch made it desirable to keep the center of the floor unobstructed, the lower half of the newly added windows was covered with

striped cotton café curtains (shades on the upper half screen out strong afternoon sun), so that the furniture could be arranged against the walls. This is kept to a minimum—a table and chairs for meals or games, twin studio couches for seating and putting up overnight guests, plastic and wrought-iron shelves and tables—the desk table, an inspired improvisation, is no more than a plastic-surfaced top on an old, white-painted sewing machine base. The

smaller pieces of furniture are light enough to be moved out of the way when a party is in progress, and the noticeable absence of clutter keeps the room looking tidy. The sole note of luxury is the stone fireplace, a thoughtful addition since remodeled sun porches are notoriously hard to heat.

If the carefree country character of this room and the simplicity of the furnishings give a clear indication of the style of the house and the preferences of the people who live there, the same is certainly true of this totally different family room—also a made-over sun porch but with a decidedly contemporary, much more adult aspect. In this case, the original outlines of the porch have been extended and enclosed with fixed and sliding panels of glass. The floor, which looks like hand-pegged random planking, is actually a stock flooring of cypress that can be bought ready made. To make the new room seem less a tacked-on addi-

the tailored Roman shades, repeated in the upholstery of the love seat, is in pleasant contrast to the abstract geometrics of the Moroccan rug and the leopard-printed plastic upholstery of the small chairs around the game table. Silhouetted against the glass, the varying styles and shapes of the furniture are also played off against one another: a straight-lined sofa, upholstered to the floor, contrasts with the curving, wrought-iron frame of the love seat, a square parquet-topped coffee table is

tion than a permanent part of the original house plan, beams were added to the acoustical tile ceiling, and the area leading to the kitchen and dining room, where the bar, stereo system, storage cabinets and bookshelves are located, was paneled with chestnut in a natural, warm-toned brown. The body of the room, washed with light throughout the day and illuminated by ceiling spots at night, is enlivened by a subtle counterpoint of color, pattern and texture. The dotted and striped linen of

set off by a circular lamp table and the cushiony contours of that classic of contemporary design, the Eames lounge chair. As much a second living room as a family gathering place, the converted sun porch is comfortable without being conventional, and manages to fit into one not-too-large area, without overcrowding or chaos, all the accouterments of leisure living. In short, it represents all the best attributes of a new and praiseworthy addition to the roster of American rooms.

ROOM FOR A CHANGE–
THE CONSTANTLY UPDATED KITCHEN

SMALL wonder that the kitchen queens it over the rest of the house. Not only is a large share of the building budget—an estimated $5,000 to $10,000—lavished on the kitchen, but even after this initial outlay it remains the room most likely to be remodeled. The metamorphosis of the kitchen has been like that of ugly duckling to swan. Before the disappearance of domestic help, kitchens were strictly utilitarian rooms for professional cooks, furbished with little more than a sink, range, refrigerator, cabinets and possibly a worktable. They might be cozy in a homely old-shoe sort of way, but they were seldom decorated and never chic. Once the woman of the house took over her own kitchen and spent the greater part of each day there, this backwardness was immediately remedied. The advent of plastics and colored cooking equipment heralded the reign of the push-button paradise. Overnight every kitchen worth its salt blossomed with pink, blue or yellow ranges, refrigerators and freezers, vivid laminated plastic countertops and vinyl tile floors. Pots, pans and casseroles, also converts to color, came out of their hiding places in cabinets to be displayed on walls.

As solid walls gave way to the revealing openplan, the kitchen shared space with and often overshadowed the living room or family room. Inevitably, the dining room waned as the kitchen waxed. Dining areas, snack counters and breakfast nooks in the new come-hither kitchen absorbed many of the duties of the dining room. While the rapturous love affair with color ran its course, kitchen decoration was on strictly contemporary lines with a preponderance of sleek surfaces— enamel and tile, chrome, steel and plastic. This in turn gave way to a more furnished, living-room look, with wallpapers and fabrics, suitably treated to resist stains and moisture, paintings and murals, accessories both pertinent and irrelevant covering every part of the kitchen not given over to equipment. When the vogue for natural textures was at its height, the kitchen was often faced with wood (real rather than the wood-grain plastics), brick and stone, ceramic tile and terrazzo.

The increasing variety and decentralization of major equipment, which made it possible to sink a cooking top in a tile counter or put a freezer in a paneled wall, brought another type of kitchen decoration into being. There were French Provincial and Early American kitchens, where modern wall ovens and refrigerators rubbed shoulders with wood paneling and Franklin stoves. The national adoption of gourmet cooking, with every man a *bon vivant*, spawned a spate of epicurean kitchens where out-in-the-open, artful arrangements of esoteric implements and ingredients and a black iron restaurant-size range promised (but did not always deliver) gastronomic delights. Although it is unlikely that kitchens will ever stabilize at any particular style, there has been a refreshing return of late to a clean-cut, straightforward simplicity well suited to the nature of the room. The kitchen opposite, colorful but not insistent, lively without being distracting, typifies this more direct decoration. The flat reflective surfaces of the walls and the doors of the cabinets and refrigerator are given dimension by a sheath of cane-printed Formica, while smaller-scale real cane laminated in clear vinyl covers the floor. The single, permissible touch of extravaganza is a bar cabinet of screen-printed Formica that conjures up an imaginary eighteenth-century tropical landscape.

Both artists and chefs prefer to bring cooking utensils out in the open rather than to conceal them in cabinets. To an artist, the form and texture of an object is justification enough. To a chef, his *batterie de cuisine* must be easy to reach. The vogue for

hanging pots and pans, baskets and boards, copper molds and wire whisks on the kitchen wall may have arisen partly for reasons of aesthetics or accessibility, but more probably from the need to get some of the clutter out of the cabinets and from

a desire to make an impersonal, modern kitchen more individual. The wall display above, left hints that the owner is both an amateur chef and a collector with a flair for design. In the kitchen above—too narrow at that point to accommodate cabinets—the arrangement is motivated more by lack of elbow room, although by dint of putting a wood frame around the panel of perforated hardboard, the arrangement of copper molds, tankards and saucepans also qualifies as decoration.

New designs in major cooking equipment did more than anything to change the face of the American kitchen. With the separation of the range into two distinct entities—oven and surface cooking units—and the introduction of cooking islands and counters, the kitchen was freed from the confines of four solid walls and able to move right out into the embrace of the open plan. The kitchen of the fifties had good reason to be dubbed the hub or heart of the house. Wives who had formerly cooked in solitude now made meals in company, with guests or family conveniently isolated on the far side of a work counter but still in talking range. Heat, steam and the smell of cooking were quickly drawn out and dispelled by powerful fans situated in the ceiling or in hoods over the cooking area.

Once the kitchen was no longer closed off, it began to look less like a kitchen and more like a living room. Cabinets were fashioned after the style of wood furniture, faced with walnut and teak veneers or plastic facsimiles, and raised off the floor on slender metal legs. The part of the kitchen in full view tended to be more decorative than functional, with prominent pieces of equipment, such as wall ovens, dishwashers, refrigerators and freezers discreetly concealed. In the kitchen opposite and below, part of one big open room for dining and cooking, the first impression is of a long sweep of space from the window wall at the front of the house to an obscure glass wall at the back, which opens to a small garden off the kitchen. There is no sudden switch in decoration: the same vinyl floor tile is used throughout, and a storage wall and travertine wall continue from one side of the cooking counter to the other. The placement of the equipment makes it virtually unnoticeable: cooking top and sink flush with the L-shaped counter and the wall oven, refrigerator and freezer built in opposite each other at either side of the sliding door (a neat way of adding extra wall space to an area that has very little). As the outer surface of the built-ins is left bare, only the plants in the patio and a glass-fronted storage cabinet are directly in line with the dining table.

Once kitchens broke away from the convention that cooking belongs in a room of its own, they began to invade and often influence the decoration of the living room or family room. Actually, these living kitchens, as they came to be called, were nothing more than a reversion to the old-style kitchen of Colonial days, where the family hearth was also the cook's domain. Whereas then the motivation was undoubtedly the need for warmth and comfort (the kitchen being the only well-heated room in the house), the new style of living kitchen sprang from an equally practical desire to conserve and gain space by concentrating the bulk of the family's home life in one large, attractive open-plan room. The kitchen opposite has most of the attributes of a family room—library, television, a dining table and chairs—and can function as such on a part-time basis. The kitchen above goes even further by actually being part of a completely furnished family room, with the cooking area marked off by an island assembly of cabinets braced by slim but strong aluminum supports, open on four sides to speed the preparation and serving of meals. In both cases, the decoration of the room is determined by the contemporary style of the cabinets and the sleek practical materials.

ROOMS THAT GET DOWN TO BUSINESS— THE HOME STUDIO AND OFFICE

WHILE certain rooms of long standing got lost in the space shuffle, others with practically no precedent but a particular application for twentieth-century living took their place. These new rooms—or demi-rooms as many of them were— revealed a great deal about the changes that had come over the country since the turn of the century. The emergence of a new kind of home-based professional class, the increasing pressure of paperwork on businessmen, a tax structure that allowed a certain amount of bona fide domestic office space to be written off, increased leisure, and a growing interest in the arts and creative crafts were related aspects of this sudden but not surprising change.

In the days when America was a young and striving nation, single-mindedly dedicated to industrial development and the pursuit of happiness through honest toil, it would have been unthinkable for anyone but a rich dilettante or a starving artist to have a studio, anyone but a merchant prince or a struggling doctor to need an office in his home. In fact, it was only recently that anything other than the home workshop, cradle of a do-it-yourself movement now happily passed into oblivion, was really sanctioned as a free-time retreat. But as the work week shortened, as more labor-saving appliances were spawned each season, and as the national income rose, it soon became apparent that there had to be something more challenging than carpentry for idle hands to do. Creativity became a virtue. Those who had never before put brush to canvas or hand to loom discovered that the world of arts and crafts was open to everyone, not only the esoteric few. The stock of the once-ridiculed Sunday painters (whose company, after all, included two of the world's most admired statesmen)

soared, and art stores did a booming business. In the ten years between 1950 and 1960, the ranks of artists and art teachers gained over 20,000 new recruits, a good part of them men. The aspiring artist's gear, once crowded in a corner of the closet along with baseball bats and picnic baskets, was now brought out into the open and allowed to take over part of the family room or an empty attic. In rare cases where art was a full-time avocation rather than a weekend hobby the studio might be a separate structure built at a quiet remove from the house. Wherever it was located, the new type of home studio was less likely to be a romantic higgledy-piggledy atelier than a well-organized workroom like the one opposite, which shares space with a family room. Taking advantage of the flagged floor and vast skylight, this studio occupies one end of the room and is sensibly equipped with a wall of built-in storage, where working materials can be neatly filed and shut away when the room is needed for family activities.

Not all home studios harbor painters. Some are offices for the new professional classes—designers, interior decorators, architects, commercial artists and writers—who either operate as free lances or carry work home with them at nights and weekends. Such studios, which usually include a drafting board or worktables, files, bookshelves and essential tools and reference materials of the trade, are of necessity a semipermanent part of the house, all set up and ready to operate at a moment's notice. This state of being constantly on view requires that, whatever the nature of the work, the home studio or office should be smoothly integrated with the rest of the house through decoration, or given privacy and an identity of its own by

screening devices. In many cases, the elements of work in progress supply the decoration. A fabric designer may arrange colorful spools of fibers and yarns on shelves, an architect can pin his blueprints and sketches on the wall. In the living-room-cum-studio at left the drawing board, prop for an industrial designer's projects, is painted faux bois fashion, stuck with sketches and swatches so that it seems more like a trompe l'œil painting than a work surface. The other serviceable piece of furniture, a really large desk, has an antique charm that takes it out of the office category. Although the background of tailored Roman shades, vinyl tile floor and plain walls is undistracting for daytime work, it looks equally inviting when the room is turned over to evening entertaining.

The studio opposite, on the other hand, makes no pretense to be other than it is, a professional but attractive sanctum for a woman who is in business as a design consultant. Studio-type slanting windows are softened by shirred Austrian curtains, the severity of the starkly modern steel-and-glass worktable offset by graceful eighteenth-century pull-up chairs and the built-in cabinets for samples and records blended into the walls by the matching facing of heavy gray linen. Cabinet-top space by the desk holds a light box for viewing transparencies, shelves slide out beneath the counter for the typewriter, telephone and note pads. This home studio, planned down to the last detail—a practical but attractive lighting fixture—succeeds in combining femininity with complete efficiency.

Limited space is no hindrance nowadays to anyone in need of an office at home. Free-standing room-divider walls like the one at the left can be set up anywhere to provide the essentials of seclusion and storage. Here the wall unit screens off one end of the living room to give an architect elbow room for drafting board and files, display space for his work, and a shelf for two telephones.

In a clear exposition of Parkinson's Law, as automation increased the country's leisure hours the actual free time of the executive and professional classes decreased because, while income rose to an all-time high, the amount of paperwork required to sustain it increased in almost the same ratio. Businessmen, even those comparatively low on the company totem pole, now spend most of their working days in conferences or on jet planes on their way to more conferences, and carry home at nights and weekends a brief case full of unfinished business. Add to this the complexities of an internal revenue system that requires every man (and

woman) to be his own bookkeeper, and it was inevitable that home, once a refuge from the cares of the day, should become the abode of the adding machine and the electric typewriter. With a steady accumulation of tax data and documentation added to the normal accumulation of unpaid bills and unanswered letters, a desk, often supplemented by a filing cabinet, today comes under the heading of necessary equipment for a well-ordered house.

Like the home studio, the office-at-home ranges from a desk in the corner of the living room, smoothly blended with the other furnishings (like the one at the left), to a screened-off area or an out-and-out room. Fortunately, there are desks to agree with any type of interior decoration from

ment shown left, the office takes over a few square feet of the foyer and is shielded from the living room by an ingenious room divider of framed sections of sliced-off bamboo, a device that hides the desk but still allows light to filter through. Paradoxically, while more houses acquire office space, the actual business office is being decorated to look just like home. Executive suites, once the stern surroundings of captains of industry, are now hung with modern paintings, swaddled in deep carpets and silk draperies, furnished with seductively contoured chairs and couches, and might well be called not business offices but business living rooms.

French Provincial and Louis XVI to Early American and the sleekest contemporary designs. Small rooms or apartments can be fitted with wall units, either ready made or built-in, where the desk is incorporated with storage. In desperate cases, where there is no room for both a desk and a dining table, the wider-than-average table-desk is an apt solution. In the office at the right, the desk is homemade, a simple wooden slab mounted on painted file cabinets. Although this office is stripped to the bare essentials, a fanciful touch of toy animals on the bookshelves relieves its dedicated severity.

As few homes can afford this luxury of a full-fledged office, the usual procedure is to pre-empt part of another room for desk detail. In the apart-

ROOMS THAT WORK AROUND THE CLOCK–
STUDIO APARTMENTS AND SUITES

A SINGULAR product of the twentieth century that has become as familiar and accepted as transistor radios and tranquilizers (to cite two widely dissimilar examples) is the room that remains on camera twenty-four hours a day. These all-purpose rooms, as they were at one time called, range from the one room in a house that, by virtue of having no specific function, frequently performs a great many (as guest-room-cum-study-cum-sitting-room) to the kind of minimum apartment loosely described as a studio. More and more people, in these high-rent days, are committed to living in one room, either because they are young and money-conscious, or older and desirous of a city pied-à-terre as a companion to a country residence.

The amount of one-room living that goes on in America, clearly indicated by the floors of studio apartments in new high-rise buildings, has engendered a category of furnishings designed to conserve space and prevent the claustrophobic feeling of living in an overcrowded closet. Dual-purpose furniture, such as the day bed and convertible sofa, can be found in all styles and materials, from the elegant small-scale beds of the eighteenth century to large cushiony contemporary sofas that hide in their capacious depths a double bed. Tables ambiguous enough in appearance to serve also as desks, wall-storage systems, free-standing room dividers, units that put into one neat package of chests and cabinets a place for everything from clothes and linens to TV and bar storage, and the handy little combination table-benches are just a few of the current crop of furnishings designed for those who have to fit a lot of living into a home that may be little larger than a decent-sized hotel room. Heavy, space-swallowing furniture has been out-lawed from these modern minimum homes in favor of the kind that is lightly scaled and off-the-floor, and the solid club chair has given way to small, easily movable chairs that can be switched from conversation group to dining table to TV corner.

The room opposite, an attic converted into a luxurious little suite, sums up many of the fine points of large living in small space. One end, allotted to seating, dining, books and cooking, has a few well-chosen pieces of furniture, all of which do double duty: the sofa as a bed, the red lacquer table as a desk and the side chairs and armchair for dining or conversation. The red-and-yellow color scheme accented with deep blue is strong enough to make the room look cheerful and lively, simple enough to pull it together (too many colors in too small a space can only result in confusion). One whole wall is fitted with a neat, space-saving arrangement of built-in bookshelves and the modern compact decentralized kitchen equipment that has replaced the old unsightly line-up known as the Pullman kitchen. Completely faced with Formica, some of it screen-printed to match the printed fabric on the sofa and chairs, the two-part kitchen and bar is attractive and harmonious enough to be left in full view, although, to hide the aftermath of a meal or shut out the odors of cooking, it can be closed off with screens of wood-grain Formica that blend with the façade of the bookshelves, giving the appearance of a storage wall. While this top-of-the-house retreat actually exists as an extra entertaining room for small cocktail and supper parties or as a suite designed to allow a guest or relative independence, it has the adroit space engineering common to the one-room efficiency apartments from which the bulk of the ideas shown here are derived.

When one room plays many parts, there has to be some slight but significant distinction between areas, sufficient at least to provide a change of pace when moving from one to the other. Screens and room dividers, chests placed back to back with sofas, and area rugs are a few of the decorative devices resorted to as a means of marking off invisible boundaries within a room. In the studio apartment below, an example of the austerely uncluttered look in one-room living, a light-colored area rug indicates the line of demarcation between the seating group and the storage-and-sleeping

sector. An updated version of that space-hoarding standby, the Murphy bed, discreetly concealed by day in the storage wall, is screened at night from the foyer by a pull-across accordion-fold door.

The daytime office and nighttime bedroom above also relies on a rug, in this case gaily patterned and tasseled, to draw the line between the two functions of the room. Apart from this, the decoration is smoothly synchronized throughout by a saffron-and-red color scheme. Even the file cabinet (a night table after working hours) is painted to echo in reverse the colors of the felt bedcover.

Contemporary furniture and one-room apartments might have been made for each other. The sleek, structural lines of today's steel-framed chairs and tables seem expressly designed for the studio apartment (in this case, literally both studio and apartment) shown opposite and below. That the room is more fully furnished than first appears is due both to the absence of bulk in the slim, see-through lines of the metal chairs, coffee tables, worktable and floor-to-ceiling storage unit, and the fact that the two really heavy pieces of furniture, the bed and the red leather sofa, are built into wall niches. The bed, constructed like a bunk with storage drawers underneath, can also be completely closed off by folding screens. The long narrow apartment is made to seem wider by a neutral color scheme, a vinyl tile floor laid like horizontal planking and the mirrors that back the sofa and white dining table. As this is an apartment for work as well as for relaxation, color is minimized, concentrated on the bed, red-covered in a red niche, and the sofa, with small changeable accents here and there. Like many such interiors, this extremely modern apartment derives most of its appeal and individuality from the interplay of shapes: the angularity of the steel and leather chairs contrasting with the padded contours of the tufted sofa and the amusing eccentric curves of a horn chair.

ROOM TO GROW IN–A CHILD'S WORLD FROM INFANCY ON

IF THE family room reflects the modern family, the child's room certainly mirrors that lively phenomenon, the modern child. Like the child, it is bright and busy, rugged and realistic and as relentlessly up to date as a space capsule. Today the child's private world is not just a copy of the adult's, cut down to size, but as sensibly and suitably furnished as any room in the house. Take the nursery. Once a nursery, by definition, was a frilly pink-and-white or blue-and-white bower with a ruffled bassinet and curtains, a romanticized background for an infant to whom ribbons and bows were to grab and chew. Cribs and chests were stenciled with whimsical animals, under the mistaken impression that this would charm baby's immature and unfocused eye. No modern nursery would give such objects house room. Now the nursery is trim, sleek and workmanlike, with an easy-to-clean floor and washable shades or painted shutters that do a better job of screening light for afternoon naps than the old organdy curtains.

The nursery opposite, planned from the outset to keep pace with a growing child, is practically one hundred per cent plastic. Plastic faces the ends of the crib, the chests, counter tops and toy shelves. Vertical louvered shades, a pint-sized rocking chair (a scaled-down version of the molded Bertoia chair) and the bed, which will take over once the room's small occupant has outgrown the crib, come in the plastic category and the floor takes yet another form—vinyl tile. The soft yellow-and-white color scheme, good at any age, and the absence of childish props (except for toys) ensure that the room can go from infancy to adolescence virtually unchanged. The improvement in children's furniture has come fairly recently, as designers noted the dearth of flexible furnishings that would conform to a child's rapidly changing needs and absorb plenty of hard knocks during the young-savage stage (the natural violence of youth, inhibited indoors for years, is now accepted as a necessary if nerve-racking part of growing up and accordingly allowed for). This new furniture is simple, straightforward, and unadorned, on the logical assumption that any decorative flourishes will be supplied by toys, games, finger paintings and other assorted belongings. Stacking units and chests, storage walls and even beds are designed to adapt to rising age levels. The idea that a bedroom should be a room for repose has no place in a young and vigorous life. Children's high tolerance for color and noise makes it possible and practical to indulge in vivid, gay color schemes based on paintable furniture, washable curtains, rugs and bedspreads and hard, durable surfaces. As a child's bedroom frequently has to fill in as a bad-weather playroom, the floor space is kept as free and unhampered as possible for active games, and there is always a large worktable or counter for cutting and pasting, painting and jigsaw puzzles. Although no child can be considered naturally tidy, shelves and big wicker hampers for toys go a long way toward initiating good habits, and a blackboard or cork pin-up board helps to keep the walls from being scrawled on.

Where two children have to share a room, the touchy sense of ownership is taken into account by a duplication of everything that could possibly be claimed, from a row of shelves to a fair share of counter-top space. Small wonder that the child of today should be considered privileged—but privileged for a purpose, to encourage him to take pride and interest in his own world in miniature.

Furniture that bridges the awkward interim stages in a child's life has happily eliminated the in-between room, obviously outdated but still in a period of uneasy transition. It would be difficult to pinpoint the actual age of the occupant of the room opposite. The only indications of his fledgling state are the Danish child's chair, a cleverly designed piece of molded plywood with a seat that adjusts to five heights, and the nature of the toys. The plastic-topped play table, storage chests and full-size bed, although presently at a level slightly lower than normal (screw-in legs will elevate them gradually) are suitable for any but the tenderest years. The background also dispenses with any overt signs of infancy. Bed and cushions are covered with scarlet and fawn corduroy, the rug is a matching scarlet and fawn stripe, the walls soft off-white. Glass-matted pictures slipped into a double

track of picture molding on the walls can be changed to keep up with juvenile interests, notoriously fickle.

The two-part room above deals just as directly with an even trickier situation—fair division of one space between two boys of different ages and enthusiasms. Although the two halves of the room share a common blue, yellow and white color scheme and almost identical furniture, each reveals a distinct and separate identity. Cover-up shades screening the storage wall and window on the smaller boy's side are painted with big, bold simple designs while the older boy has shades that show a more grown-up map of the world. The zigzag pattern of the vinyl tile floor draws a firm demarcation line, reinforced by a room divider that gives privacy without blocking light and a swinging door, marked with joking but firm finality.

In the perpetual battle waged between parents and teen-age daughters over the sloppy state of juvenile bedrooms, one salient fact is likely to be overlooked. It is infinitely easier for a teen-ager to put things away when she has a logical and orderly place to put them. The organizational opportunities afforded by a storage wall are virtually unlimited. Not only can it swallow the overflow from closets and chests but it can also supply desk space for study and a permanent place for the essential television and a phonograph.

The storage wall in the girl's room above is not merely built-in, it is foresightedly soundproofed by a urethane foam backing bonded to the printed fabric that covers the wall. The record player

against which this baffle is directed reposes tidily in the center drawers, and the speakers are unobtrusively set in flush with the shelves at the top of the wall. For pajama parties, benches padded with foam rubber and covered in the same print pull out from under the counter top. While the shelves and cork pin-up boards on the wall opposite represent a much simpler construction, they can be augmented, should the need arise, by more shelves and wall units hooked onto the standards, and extra chests of drawers fitted into the space under the desk counter top. In a further concession to teen-age interests, a full-length mirror and vanity shelf, lighted, theatrical fashion, by strong downlights, are built into a recess by the windows.

ROOMS THAT GET AWAY FROM IT ALL—
THE PERSONAL BEDROOM, THE PERFECT GUEST ROOM

A GLANCE at the present-day bedroom is sufficient to establish it as the most personal room in the house and the one least likely to be affected by any temporary fads and fancies of decoration. However conformist we may be in the more public aspects of our private lives, when it comes to bedrooms we are rugged individualists. There are bedrooms as chaste as a monastic cell, although considerably more luxurious, like the bedroom opposite. Bare-floored and bare-walled it may be, but a fur throw, upholstered headboard and footboard and a well-padded leather chair hardly come under the heading of asceticism. The dark neutral tones of the color scheme and the few decorative objects, each in its own way beautiful to look at, reveal a desire for privacy and restful surroundings. Then there is the extroverted bedroom, occupied all day long. Here the essential bed and chest are supplemented by a desk or table for answering mail, a cozy armchair and bookshelves, and the decoration is light, bright and cheerful. Some people, shunners of the day, like their bedrooms to resemble dim cavelike retreats. They upholster the walls and shroud the windows to keep out sound and light, and have revived the cloistered calm of the canopied wall bed and the French lit clos. Other bedrooms, whose owners are advocates of the window wall and communion with nature, open to a sun-bathing terrace.

Devotees of gadgets equip their bedrooms with television and stereo that can be switched around by remote control, and push-button systems that start the coffee perking, open the draperies or run up the flag on the front lawn. Collectors who fear for their treasures relegate them to their bedrooms where they are safe and can be savored in solitude.

Look and you can find almost anything in bedrooms today, from reducing machines and mechanized beds to modern paintings and built-in bars —but almost never the old bedroom suite of matched night tables, chests and beds. Today no one with an ounce of originality would allow one inside the bedroom door. Instead, the bed may be a four-poster, the chest an antique semainier and the night stand a small marble-topped coffee table. Not only the style but also the size of bedrooms has changed. The traditional chamber of moderate size has given way to either the small functional room furnished for little more than sleep, or the large and lavishly appointed master suite equipped with a fireplace, books, television, armchairs, a breakfast table and a separate dressing room.

Just as the bedroom has altered beyond all recognition, so has its opposite number, the guest room. It is hard to pinpoint—or even to find—the guest room nowadays. Like other rooms once rated as part-time luxuries, it has become lost in the changeover from rambling old houses to compact new houses and has been forced to change its character to keep up with the times. Today the guest room may be a study, sitting room or studio with a day bed tucked against one wall or even a corner of the living room that can be converted for an overnight guest by opening up the sofa. Oddly enough, this has had a tonic effect. The guest room is now infinitely more comfortable and relaxing than the old version, which had all the charm, warmth and personality of an eight-dollar-a-night hotel room. Furnished with everything from a clock radio to a place to write letters in peace, the guest room is in many respects undistinguishable from or even more luxurious than the bedroom.

As bedrooms diminished in size they became much more attractive, a virtue that compensated for the lack of elbow room. Walls covered with paper or fabric, vinyl tile floors and accent rugs, imaginative wall treatments and shapely accessories all helped to make them seem more furnished, but it was left to the bed, by reason of its dominant size, to take over the burden of decoration. No longer was a simple boxspring and mattress cloaked in a basic bedspread considered adequate. Plain beds were made beautiful by the addition of brass, wicker, wood and wrought-iron headboards; bedhead walls were set off from the rest of the room with paint, paper or a panel of fabric. The elegant canopied and poster beds of the eighteenth and nineteenth centuries were revived, modified in scale and painted in luscious contemporary colors. Their soaring vertical lines,

like those of the half-canopied bed opposite, did much to make the room seem airier and more spacious, by directing the eye upward. So did the alcove bed, tucked away in a draped wall niche to leave floor space free for an armchair and an occasional table. Covered and curtained with a toile that matches the wallpaper, the alcove bed above virtually fades into the background. Less like modern bedrooms than old-fashioned boudoirs,

these beguilingly feminine rooms are responsible for restoring another time-honored custom to everyday usage—the establishment of a bedroom desk as the household headquarters where bills are paid, menus planned and the activities of the forthcoming week mapped out. As every desk must have a chair comfortable enough to encourage reflection, the bedroom also is earmarked as a retreat for catching up on the latest best-seller.

113

With the change in bedrooms came a corresponding change in beds. According to the style and size of the room, it was possible to choose from a positive wealth of beds, starting with the minimum thirty-inch studio couch barely wide enough for a restless string bean, and culminating in a mammoth eighty-incher, more emperor- than king-size, and—what was equally important to find bedding made to measure. The innocuous twin beds which for ostensible reasons of hygiene (more likely, a desire to be considered up-to-date) had replaced the good old-fashioned double bed in the twenties and thirties now, in turn, fell out of favor. In their place were beds that really looked as if they belonged in a bedroom, like the billowy canopied bed in the flowery traditional room opposite, or the severe but handsome double bed with tailored felt cover and cane headboard in the study-guest-room below. Beyond doubt, the bed has re-established itself as the master of all it surveys.

The duality of the present-day guest room—furnished half for the family, half for the guest—is clearly revealed in its decoration. Often the need for such a room is the impetus for a long-overdue remodeling. This was the case with the guest room above, originally an attic. Although it extends all the courtesies of a guest room—a built-in bed with drawers below for extra blankets, a roomy chest, a table for a breakfast tray and

plenty of books to while away insomniac hours plus a decent light by which to read them—the materials and furnishings are obviously destined for harder wear than they will ever receive from the occasional guest. The wood-grain vinyl laid over the original floorboards, the walls covered in a dark patterned fabric that will not show finger marks, the padded window seat and the floor cushions that take the place of chairs can easily

116

withstand day-in, day-out use by the family, even the teen-agers, for whom this makes a secluded spot in which to roll up the rug and dance.

The more elegant room below is just as definitely intended for adult relaxation, with or without the benefit of a visitor. The decoration here owes a great deal to the Brighton Pavilion, that English Regency folly responsible for the vogue for bamboo furniture that still prevails today. Not only the whimsical lines of the bamboo bed, bolstered for daytime seating comfort, and the Chinese-style fretwork backs and sides of the open-arm chairs recall the Prince Regent's flight of fancy, but also the orange and yellow printed fabric that covers the bed and walls, an adaptation of the Pavilion's paisley canopy. Although the net effect might be tiring in a bedroom, it is perfectly suited to a room that sees only occasional service.

That the present-day decoration of bedrooms is first and foremost a statement of personal taste is self-evident. How else would it be possible to reconcile two such utterly dissimilar examples as the bedrooms above and opposite? About the only thing they have in common is a bed and a bedhead treatment designed to draw attention to it. From there on the divergence is marked. The bedroom above is stark and simple, predominantly neutral and decorated mainly by the interaction of different tones of wood, from light to dark, used for the furniture, on the floor and end wall. The bed, a mattress on a wrought-iron and wood frame, is distinguished solely by the bedhead backing, a wall of built-in storage with open shelves. Book jackets and two soft orange accent pillows on the bed are the only noticeable touches of color in a

room designed primarily for repose. The muted serenity and severity of this room is in complete contrast to the bedroom opposite, a wild mélange of Victorian Gothic, Oriental and modern that is about as far out as anyone would think of going in bedroom decoration. The bed is actually a pallet, a mattress set on a tatami-covered platform with a closed-up Victorian mahogany fireplace as a headboard. Although this room, on examination, is found to contain all the essentials (a bed, table, chairs and a chest) as well as such added flourishes as plants and paintings, in every other respect it is unorthodox, a revelation of the owner's flair for color and pattern and overriding sense of fun, for the original interior, heavy with beams and paneling, has been left untouched, lightened only by paper, paint and imagination.

118

ROOM FOR INDULGENCE–
THE ELEGANT, ULTIMATE BATHROOM

NO MATTER how prosaic its function, a beautiful bathroom always carries a connotation of sybaritic pleasure. This may be a matter of association with the ancient Romans and their luxurious marble baths—or it may be due to the fact that until the middle of the nineteenth century, a bathroom complete with all the appurtenances was owned by only a few of the wealthier American families. A late arrival among rooms, the bathroom is still enough of a luxury to encourage its owners to spend an inordinate amount of money on its trappings, and even a Caesar might goggle at the sight of the elaborate bathroom of today. Frequently the most lavish room in the house, the bathroom revels in gold faucets and marble tubs, wallpaper and wall-to-wall carpeting, telephones and Impressionist paintings, built-in sun lamps and saunas, and even, in those regions where the climate cooperates, a private terrace.

Today's bathroom is seldom a single entity. Most houses now have not one but two or three bathrooms and the one-bathroom family is becoming almost as extinct as the one-car family, although presumably both still exist. As befits its lofty status, the master bathroom has the edge over those smaller bathrooms set aside for children or guests. These are often tiny cubicles containing little more than a lavatory, toilet and shower, on the sensible assumption that there is no call to squander the plumbing and that anyone who wants to immerse himself in hot water can always take over the tub. The master bathroom also boasts two lavatories, if only one of everything else. (The bidet, an essential feature of the European bathroom, has yet to make much headway in America and is, indeed, unlawful in certain states.) Although

the built-in look that prevails today might seem the latest thing in bathroom design, it is not new at all. The Victorians, who put skirts on everything, including pianos, concealed the inner workings of their baths, wash-basins and toilets in vast expanses of marble and mahogany. It was left to the health faddists of a later date to expose the pipes and lift the tub off the floor on claw feet in a determined search for dirt and germs. But where the Victorians doted on heavy, dark wood we surround our bathroom fixtures with light, bright and practical materials, ceramic tile, plastic, marble, terrazzo and light wood veneers, and although many of our sinks are wall-hung and sunk in cantilevered counter tops there is not a pipe in sight.

Undoubtedly the greatest change in the face of the bathroom came with the rage for color. There was a time when bathrooms were shining, spanking white—white tile floor and walls, white tub, sink and toilet, white towels and shower curtains, white soap, very pure, very clinical and very cold. But as with kitchens, so with bathrooms—once color took hold, it soon took over. Although at first the most popular colors were pallid pastels, the timid quickly gained heart, and with the proliferation of the new colorful plastics the bathroom blossomed like a garden. Walls were covered with patterned papers treated to resist moisture and splashes, rugs and washable cotton carpeting took over the floor, and towels and shower curtains ran the gamut both of pattern and the palette. No one nowadays would blink an eyelash at a bathroom like the one opposite with its riot of red and white marbleized paper, its red rug and curtains and its white tile floor and lavatories—for white is still needed to keep color in its place.

The innovation that did most to bring order to the bathroom and eliminate family morning bottlenecks was the wall-to-wall counter. This neat package deal of lavatories, dressing table and storage cabinets backed by mirrors had the additional advantage of good lighting, an attribute noticeably lacking in bathrooms of the past. In the sleek ceramic tile bathroom above, a luminous ceiling sheds light through plastic panels on the counter of wall-hung wood cabinets and a smaller cabinet (a modern version of the medicine chest) under the mirror. In the bathroom opposite, a luxury affair with marble tub and counter top, gold and crystal faucets, wall-to-wall carpeting and a mosaic mural, the counter lighting is recessed in a cove behind an egg-crate grille of plastic.

123

The twentieth century's major contribution to the roster of decorative structural materials, plastic brought sweeping changes to the bathroom. Colorful, lightweight and strong plastic panels were frequently set up like walls to shield one area from another or to create free-standing compartments within the bathroom. This wise trend to the compartmented bathroom, where a divider might screen off tub from toilet or one counter-top lavatory from another, heralded a welcome return to privacy, one of the intangible personal luxuries that had all but disappeared in recent years. The system of dividers was a particular boon to small bathrooms with little elbow room or storage space, adding an extra wall for shelves or towel rails. In the bathroom above left, a framed panel of vari-colored plastic neatly splits the counter in two. On one side is a lavatory and dressing table with theatrical lighting over the mirror, on the other a sink and the bath, with a towel rack in between.

Plastics proved their worth in children's bathrooms by being hardwearing and easy to clean. In the child's bath and cloakroom opposite, panels of plastic patterned with outsize polka dots are mounted on poles to mark off a wash-up area and a shower stall, glassed in on the fourth side. Cabinets, chest and benches, all plastic-surfaced and all scaled down to suit a child, can be easily and inexpensively changed when the children grow up. The decorative possibilities of plastic have been thoroughly exploited in bathrooms, especially second bathrooms where limited space and budget preclude the more extravagant effects. For instance, in the tiny bathroom above right, broad stripes of pumpkin and white plastic banding the shower stall, a pebble-pattern plastic counter top leading to a white-pebbled garden, and a see-through sculptured chair of clear plastic all help to make the minimum space seem wider, pleasanter and less confined than it actually is.

As bathrooms broke with convention, the standard fixtures of toilet, lavatory and tub changed style, shape and position. The toilet might be wall-hung rather than fixed to the floor, the contours of the lavatory basin square, round or oval, the bathtub square or round instead of rectangular. In the bathroom opposite, the tub has been shifted from its customary place against the wall to the middle of the room, with a fluffy fur rug alongside and two sprays of metal flowers flanking it like sentinels. The lavatory counter in the bathroom above has also adopted a center-of-the-room stance and an unusual semicircular shape, repeated by the surrounding sculptured rug. Almost anything can be found in the bathroom today, even, oddly enough, the sunken tub, one-time movie symbol of high living. A development of this, in a more frugal form, is the Japanese-style bath, a small ceramic-tile pit built out from the bathroom and discreetly surrounded on three sides by a walled garden.

ROOMS OF PASSING INTEREST—
THE WELCOMING HALL, THE INVITING FOYER

ONLY RECENTLY were halls and foyers really rated as rooms. The entrance hall was for long the Cinderella of decoration, seldom noticed because it was seldom noteworthy. Most halls were considered adequately equipped if there was a mirror for the arriving guest to check on his or her appearance, a chair to sit on while removing overshoes, and a table to hold mail and packages, the car keys and the dog's leash. Then, as rooms were telescoped in modern houses and apartments and every inch of available space had to be used to good effect, the hall was considered with a more discerning eye. Large halls or foyers were often furnished as temporary or even permanent dining areas or home offices. The welcome wealth of wall space was lined with storage units, bookshelves, or the paintings that had overflowed the living room. Small foyers were made more inviting with fabric-covered walls, paper or paint murals, plants and tiny pools or fountains.

The entrance, it came to be realized, was the first impression a visitor got of the house—and first impressions are apt to be lasting. As no one was going to spend much time in the hall, the decoration could be vividly colorful, dramatic or even faintly amusing, just so long as it was worth looking at. Nor was it necessary for the decoration of the hall or foyer to agree with that of the rest of the house. Often it was more telling if quite different—although not so different as to be completely out of keeping. Because few of the smaller foyers had room for much in the way of furniture, tables and chairs were frequently forgone in favor of wall, floor and ceiling treatments that, by concentrating color and pattern strictly on the surface, carried the weight of decoration. Painted moldings

and modern tapestries, Oriental rugs and strikingly patterned tile floors, lighting fixtures stronger on shape than illumination and all kinds of eye-catching accessories from antique barometers and baroque mirrors to trompe l'œil paintings and opaline collections found their way to the foyer. Exotica such as African masks usually ended up in the hallway, for want of a more appropriate setting, and the result, when deftly handled, could be both arresting and attractive. Windowless entrance halls were often surrounded by luminous walls of plastic panels lit from behind to bathe the whole area in a soft diffused glow against which plants and sculpture might be silhouetted.

Today one of the most popular and effective forms of decoration for a hallway—and certainly one of the most appropriate considering that it is, in effect, a gallery—is a display of paintings and art that encourages the passer-through to stop, look and linger before going on to other rooms. The long narrow entrance hall opposite was originally nothing more than a plaster-walled, brick-floored passageway leading from the front door to the back of the house, with rooms opening off on either side. Spot-lighted paintings, small carvings and sculptures set out from the walls on brackets, plants and a pair of ornamental antique jars turned it into a fascinating vista of colors and shapes, shadows and patterns, where every prized possession could be enjoyed without the distracting presence of furniture. Even the shaggy rug on the brick floor is there for a reason—to add a further contrast of texture. While this hallway is large, it has a tunnel-like quality that benefits from absence of clutter and the concentration of art and decorative objects on or against the walls.

The same is true, although in a totally different way, of the tiny hallway opposite, a featureless white-walled, terrazzo-floored corridor that serves to connect the entrance hall in the adjoining glass-walled gallery to the stairway. Such a minuscule space is patently impossible to furnish, although it desperately needs some element to make it less naked and chilly. The saving grace here is a gay, colorful modern tapestry, which, while essentially abstract in design, is woven in lyrical motifs that prove oddly compatible with the graceful curves of the traditional wrought-iron and crystal chandelier suspended over the stairwell.

In the majestically proportioned hallway above, art is again the replacement for furniture—with the exception of a low bookshelf under one of the oil paintings that acts as a display shelf for sculpture—but here the walls are not so much decorated by art as turned into vast frames for the abstract paintings spotlighted from above.

This is not to imply that furniture has been banished from the hallway, only that it must now have a more solid raison d'être than before. The furnished look is still in style, and furniture of intrinsically interesting shape, color and design will always merit a home in the hall, which explains why you are apt to see more antique settees and consoles, painted chairs and carved or lacquered chests there than contemporary chairs and tables. In the large traditional foyer above, a few well-chosen pieces of reproduction eighteenth- and nineteenth-century furniture are adroitly combined with modern paintings and antique accessories in the current fashion for mixing. The small and narrow hall opposite looks more furnished than it is because of a mirrored wall that reflects and intensifies the effect of the wall-hung units, and the Mondrian-like patterns of the luminous ceiling.

As America advances into the age of automation, a new leisure class
is emerging. Vacation houses are springing up all over the country,
harbors and marinas are chockablock with cabin cruisers and sailboats.
This new leisure calls for a distinct decorating style that supplies
comfort and ease of maintenance at a comparatively low cost.

DECORATING
FOR DIVERSION

SOCIAL trends develop so rapidly in the United States that yesterday's innovation is today's institution. The "second house," forecast by a transportation official as recently as 1955, is now as much a part of the contemporary scene as the skyscraper and the split-level. With more time and money on their hands than ever before, Americans are building, buying or remodeling a place in which to spend their bonus of leisure. According to taste, age and bank account this may be anything from a full-fledged vacation house earmarked for later retirement to a family-sized cabin cruiser or a pool house to supplement the latest hub of home entertaining, the swimming pool. Many second houses take the shape of the A-frame or the flat-topped box, both of which are easy and inexpensive to build because a great deal of the component parts come prefabricated. The drawback of these minimal houses is their bare-frame construction and rigid contours, which require considerable decorating ingenuity to make them appear pleasant, individual and homelike. An excellent treatment of the A-frame is seen in the room opposite, where plywood paneling was used to fill in the cavernous peak of the roof and cut it down to companionable size. The paneling, a warm rosewood tone, blends with the wood furniture and provides a rich background for art on the wall and built-in shelves. The furniture is small-scale and straight-lined, with no excessive bulk to crowd floor space. Mindful of the need for an adequate amount of seating in fairly low, cramped quarters, the owners built a conversation platform and pit, placing the coffee table in the dropped center and arranging low legless love seats and floor cushions around the perimeter. Small wood tables and a chest fitted for bar storage neatly square off the compact seating area, which is brightened and softened by silk pillows, flowers, leather-bound books and Oriental temple figures, precious but portable enough to be moved from town to the country.

THE NEW LEISURE HAS BROUGHT
DECORATION TO THE WATER'S EDGE

IN THE ERA which Stewart Holbrook has so aptly titled "The Age of the Moguls," the symbol and aquatic refuge of the rich was a yacht, and anyone naive enough to ask how much it cost to keep one demonstrably could not afford to. Today, with almost eight million boats owned by Americans, weekend cruising has become the sport of the leisure masses and boats floating vacation homes for the whole family. Not only the owners but also the interiors of the boats have undergone a sea change. New fabrics, fibers and finishes that require an absolute minimum of spit and polish are taking the place of the old costly mahogany and brass fittings that needed the full-time attention of a crew. Vinyl, an admirably adaptable synthetic,

has proved a boon to the boat owner who prefers a bright but hard-wearing, damp-and-mildew-proof form of decoration for his home life afloat.

Vinyl is used wholesale in the boat above and companion boathouse opposite—the latter, a foul-weather retreat or emergency weekend guest house. Walls between the white-painted beams in the boathouse are faced with ultramarine or blue, green and white daisy-patterned vinyl. The sofa and ottoman are upholstered in white ribbed vinyl, the chair in smooth-textured blue, and even the pillows follow suit. On the boat, the sofa and bunks are also vinyl-upholstered, and as practically all the remaining surfaces are painted, the maintenance of this sea-going weekend home is negligible.

A bird's-eye view of the United States is sufficient to confirm that we are a nation indissolubly dedicated to the pursuit of water. Swimming pools pattern the landscape, every lake and shoreside acre is lined with houses. This urge to live near the water is paralleled by an equally strong desire to live well. Hence the appearance of the pool house and beach lanai where swimmers and sunbathers can take their ease and sustenance without changing location or clothes. These outdoor rooms vary widely according to the preferences of the owners and the prevailing architecture. The pool house above, all green and white and canopied with billows of fern-printed vinyl, resembles a garden pavilion with classical overtones. The lanai opposite, roofed but open to the beach on two sides (shutters draw across at night) is completely contemporary. The common denominator is the waterproof, practical nature of the decoration. Walls are of painted brick. The pool house has a flagstone-pattern vinyl tile floor, the lanai a decklike platform of stained wood planks that can be quickly swept free of sand. All the furniture has plastic, enamel or painted finishes with the exception of a wicker storage-hamper-cum-end-table on the lanai and accessories that weather in their own way.

Although the pool as the socially favored rendezvous for outdoor leisure and entertaining reached its zenith in the kinder climes of California and the Southwest, Florida and Hawaii, pools can now be spotted in almost every part of the country. With the pool has come the poolside room, part terrace, part a natural and semipermanent adjunct to the house itself. Poolside rooms, thanks to the new breed of casual, comfortable and well-designed furniture that has come into being in the last decade, are often the last word in luxury. Hardy but unyielding redwood, once the people's choice, has given way to lightweight painted aluminum, tubular lacquered steel, plastic-coated rattan and molded Fiberglas. Seats, needless to say, are more often than not the ubiquitous vinyl, in all the patterns and colors of which vinyl is capable. The poolside pavilion above, actually a simple matter of a canopy

of striped Acrilan canvas held up by slender aluminum supports with a verdigris finish, is a sheltered outdoor extension of the living room, furnished to blend with the decoration of the interior. This elegant version of poolside ease is carried out with gracefully scrolled, white-painted iron furniture for lounging and dining, and pots of pink geraniums as portable color accents.

In contrast, the poolside room above is a clear continuation of the roof line of the house, projected toward the pool, with a completely contemporary feeling. A brilliant sunflower tapestry emblazoned on yellow sailcloth hangs over one corner of the roofed area as both sun screen and decoration. Folding, high-backed rattan chairs with removable plastic cushions can be swiftly moved from sun to shade. The pool, terrace and poolside room share a common facing of gray ceramic tiles.

THE VACATION HOUSE AS A HOLIDAY PIED-À-TERRE

VACATION houses today are as widely varied as the people who build them. At one end of the scale is the small but serviceable summer retreat, as simple as a shack although much more stylish, and at the other the out-and-out second home, lived in during the weekends all through the year. The minimal house is not to be confused with the rustic cabin of old, furnished with an ill-assorted jumble of cast-offs on the Spartan theory that as no one was going to spend much time indoors it would be folly to waste money on fixing the place up.

The present-day vacation house, although it may be no more than a flat-topped box, like the one at the right, qualifies as a comfortable, attractive and easy-to-maintain home. Though four-square, this typical small beach house is not shut in. One wall is insulated glass, screened at night by roll-down blinds, and the interior is partitioned merely by an open-shelf room divider that shields the entrance, kitchen and bathroom from view while adding an extra wall for storage, TV and books. The unfinished interior walls common to this kind of prefabricated house are faced with a durable urethane-foam-backed vinyl in a gay flower print that both insulates and soundproofs, and the floor is covered with flagstone pattern vinyl tile. The furniture is the wicker, rattan, metal and plastic kind mass-produced for casual indoor-outdoor living, lightly scaled and hardy, with zippered seat pads to soften the rigidity of the chairs. Simple studio couches, placed at right angles to divide the room for living and dining, serve for both seating and sleeping. This practical, pleasing vacation-house decoration, made possible by the inexpensive, well-designed furnishings to be found all over the country, can be seen from Maine to the Pacific Northwest.

THE VACATION HOUSE
AS A HOME AWAY FROM HOME

IN THE 1960's the second house took on a new connotation and greater stature. As Americans spent more time and money to escape from the stresses and strains of urban life to the space and solitude of the country, the second house became in many cases more luxuriously and lavishly equipped than the first. While a city apartment or suburban split-level might be regarded as a temporary expedient, the house in the country or at the beach, often bought or built with an eye to future equity or retirement as well as present pleasure, was looked on as an investment. The house shown here, nestled in the quiet of the Long Island sand dunes, is more than a vacation refuge from Manhattan. It is kept open all year round and used extensively for entertaining—which accounts for the decoration being more in the manner of the city than the shore. The high-ceilinged living room, oriented at night to a two-story brick fireplace (below) and by day toward the window wall opening to the terrace (opposite), is a sophisticated mixture of modern upholstered armchairs, a sofa in the Spanish style, eighteenth-century reproduction side chairs and open-arm chairs and a sleek contemporary dining table, silhouetted against white walls and a bare polished wood floor. At the

far end of the living room is an open-to-view modern built-in kitchen and above it a tiny eyrie of a studio, right, where the owner works on the vibrant canvases that blaze from the walls. At right angles to the living room is a glass-walled one-story bedroom wing, with each bedroom and bathroom screened by an enclosed garden or evergreens.

SPACE TO SPARE SPELLS ROOM FOR IMPROVEMENT

FEW HOUSES, unless custom-built, are designed to aid and abet the newly leisured life, and the result has been a spectacular remodeling boom as home owners turn odd spaces into the extra rooms they need. Even the carport is not overlooked, for its location by the kitchen represents the logical, often the only place for an extra dining or entertaining room. The carport opposite, superseded by a newly built garage, was inexpensively redeemed and remodeled by some structural alterations (mainly studs added to support shelves) and a lavishment of bright color. To hide the rafters,

yellow and red sailcloth was strung, Roman-shade fashion, between the newly stained beams, then the scored-cement floor was painted yellow, the walls red to match the overhead canopy.

As the carport above still shelters the car, the dining arrangement is strictly temporary. A drop-down door in the center section of a built-in storage wall links up with an extension-leaf barbecue cart to form a cooking and dining counter. Later, the door is pushed back into place, the cart rolls into the space beneath, and the director's chairs are folded flat and put away in the storage wall.

Older houses, considered good value today in terms of space, often have attics and basements, relics of a more expansive age, that positively beg for the talents of the remodeler. Basements have finally graduated from the rumpus-room stage, when a ping-pong table and a few folding chairs were considered adequate furnishing, and are now made over into family rooms of considerable charm and character where the activities are likely to be no more athletic than sipping a drink or playing a quiet game of cards. In many houses, either through modesty or a lack of affinity with the upstairs decoration, mementos of the chase or

silver cups, ribbons and awards are often relegated to the basement family room, making it a latter-day successor to the old-time trophy or gun room. The result, if treated amusingly rather than in the heavy-handed manner of the Victorians, who seldom took themselves or their achievements lightly, can be surprisingly successful. The remodeled basement above seems essentially a tongue-in-cheek assemblage of past exploits. Evidence of expert horsemanship is dispersed around the walls in company with books, paintings, television, plants, old silver and some frankly fake animal heads. The insistent nature of the wall display is offset by a muted color scheme: deep blue ceiling; white walls with black trim; an overscaled white-and-black vinyl tile floor; blue, black and white plaid Roman shade and sofa cushions (the same plaid sheathes the wall below the chair rail). Black leather built-in sofas and a modern steel chair and tables make up a comfortable conversation corner while the other half of the room is taken up by a pool table, sign of the current endeavor to restore this venerable game to a measure of respectability. The game room below started out as an ordinary featureless basement with brick walls and a cement floor, and apart from a coat of whitewash on the walls and black paint on the floor, the background is virtually unchanged. The verve and style of the room is due solely to the bold color scheme of black and white with touches of red and the safari souvenirs. African trophies, elephant tusks, zebra- and leopard-skin rugs and mounted heads of animals mingle with modern Mexican furniture, lacquer tables and white crash slipcovers the only clues that the room is a few thousand miles from Kenya.

Halfway through the twentieth century, a new cult of personality
became evident in decoration. Not since the eighteenth
century, when families with great fortunes and great taste amassed
the superb collections that were to stand so long unchallenged,
had there been such an abundance of interest in art and objects.

ART FOR
DECORATION'S SAKE

AMERICANS have always been collectors, as the houses of the past show, but no previous era can match the uninhibited expression of personal taste manifest in the eclectic possessions of today. Instead of the classic catalogued collections of the eighteenth century, or the nineteenth-century conglomerations of machine-made bric-a-brac and innocuous paintings of stags and sheep, houses are now filled with a wide-ranging assortment of art and accessories. The traditional rubs shoulders with the contemporary, the crude with the refined. Hand-made objects are prized for their form and feeling, folk art for its warm-hearted, imaginative naiveté. It was not always thus. Until fairly recently a flower painting on the bedroom wall and a pair of candlesticks and a clock on the living-room mantel were about as far as most people were prepared to go in the matter of ulterior decoration. It took a travel boom, well-publicized museum displays of arts and crafts and open-house tours of some of the more impressive private collections to bring about a general awareness of the culture of this and other countries. Even television turned out to be an amiable monster, for it exposed vast areas of suburban and rural America to the best the world had to offer. Little by little, people threw off the bonds of precedent and the shackles of convention. They developed sufficient confidence to have the courage of their own taste and convictions, to buy a modern painting or a piece of sculpture and to bring out into the light of day the things they had bought simply for pleasure—a Scandinavian weaving, a Japanese ceramic bowl, a Mexican painted candelabra. Art, once relegated to the background, became a prominent, even dominant, part of the decoration, as in the room opposite where the colors and shapes of an abstract oil and two arresting sculptures completely overshadow the furnishings. Such rooms are virtually decorated with art and the art in many cases costs a great deal more than the furniture, for it is now regarded as an investment to be enjoyed and moved from house to house, rather than as an impermanent, unimportant accessory.

It is no longer necessary to be a millionaire in order to be a collector, although it naturally helps. Museum loan services, installment buying and the proliferation of small galleries offering the works of lesser-known artists encourage the small but serious collector with more taste than money to become an investor in modern art. One offshoot of this cultural renaissance can be seen in the Bureau of Census figures for the decade between 1950 and 1960. They record an astounding rise in the ranks of artists, sculptors and art teachers from 80,779 to 104,705. Even the hardened Philistine had to acknowledge that art had arrived in America when hand-picked modern paintings were listed in the catalogue of a leading mail-order company.

Today, the old prospers along with the avant-garde. Modern houses with their vast expanses of plain plaster and glass are made to order not only for huge modern canvases but also for the majestic masterpieces of traditional European art that have found few homes outside museums since the days of castles and châteaux. The richness and depth of the superb Renaissance triptych opposite, unconventionally hung against the white-painted brick wall and high window of a restrained modern living room, is seen to better advantage in this stark interior than it would be in a traditional setting.

Decorating with art may sound easy on the surface, but it turns out to be rather more complex than hanging a picture on a wall. From a domestic viewpoint, large paintings are apt to induce a kind of museum fatigue unless the eye is free to wander from shape to shape and level to level, pausing now at a painting or piece of sculpture, next at a table-top or shelf arrangement of smaller shapely objects. The triptych opposite would have been overpowering without the light relief of a table group of simple peasant pottery and the airy bird cage in the foreground. That these objects are appropriate rather than out of place against such a

towering treasure merely goes to prove the innate relationship of beautiful things without regard to era or place of origin, a relationship that enables them to hold their own in the company of their design peers. The highly refined scrolls and screens, porcelains and bronzes of the Orient show a singular ability to adapt to new currents in decorating. One felicitous example of this survival of the fittest is seen in the living room below, where an antique six-panel Chinese screen looks as much at home in

this contemporary interior as it would have amid the more lavish elegance of an eighteenth- or nineteenth-century house. On the other hand, the immense museum-scale abstract paintings above could only be supported by a severely modern room, where the furniture is secondary in importance and utterly noncompetitive. Even the lighting is designed primarily to dramatize the paintings. Stone, metal and wood sculptures, positioned at different points and eye levels around the room effectively break the monotony of constant deep-focus viewing. Here art is the only decoration, and a change of paintings would alter, in a matter of minutes, the color scheme and the ambience of the room.

ACCESSORIES EN MASSE
LOOK BETTER THAN THEY ARE

NOT ALL collections of art and objects, however cherished, have enough intrinsic importance to stand alone. Many turn out to be mixed bags of unrelated acquisitions which, like characters in search of an author, need a strong raison d'être to bring them together. This may be a background consciously contrived to unify these decorative misfits, giving them more prominence than they would have if merely dotted around the room. In the living room opposite, a false wall of lighted niches cleverly combines a brass pendulum clock, Oriental vase, old oil painting, icon and mercury glass in a colorful arrangement with all the punch of one powerful painting. Similarly, the façade of dark planking in the room above both pulls together and sets off a scattering of large and small objects ranging from a gilded wall sconce and trumeau to bibelots and books clustered on a wood chest and table.

A less ambitious way to draw attention to art and accessories (and a favorite decorative stratagem today) is to group them on unoccupied wall space above the largest and most inescapable piece of living-room furniture—the sofa. Over-the-sofa arrangements are relatively easy to handle as the size and shape of the furniture virtually dictates the grouping. In the living room below, twin sofa beds take over one corner, and the walls above them are filled in to ceiling height with massed paintings and sketches. A large oil in a heavily carved frame is hung at the right to anchor and terminate the arrangement. In the sitting room opposite, striped wallpaper matched to the fabric of draperies and sofa upholstery unifies the rather limited selection of old paintings and accessories over the sofa. But here, where a traditionally balanced arrangement might be expected, the informal balance of the grouping, more often seen in contemporary rooms, brings the subject matter up to date.

Not all wall arrangements depend on furniture. Some of the most striking take up, on adjustable shelves, the entire space from floor to ceiling in an intricate composition of intriguingly shaped objects interspersed with art, books, and panels of color. These artful and expert arrangements dominate a room to such an extent that they frequently qualify as the major element in the decoration.

COLLECTORS' COMPOSITIONS–
A FORM OF ART THROUGH ARRANGEMENT

PEOPLE who collect things also like to show them off, usually in a massed wall or shelf arrangement where the collection is grouped with infinite patience and considerable expertise into a harmonious composition. The mélange of objects opposite, diversified in shape and character, is silhouetted against a white wall with a wonderful feeling for balance and design (even the squiggly wrought-iron chair backs are worked in). Situated in a small hallway, it cries out for closer inspection. An equally well-balanced, though simpler, grouping of pictures and prints above is hung on a six-panel screen in front of a window, rather than on a wall, a device that artfully saves space.

No matter how precious, perfect or rare they may be, small works of art tend to be overlooked unless concentrated in one place. Once this would have been a vitrine or china cabinet. Now they are brought out into the open where they can be seen, touched and enjoyed. In the room above, a line-up of campaign chests and a grasscloth-covered wall display miniature sculptures from several countries and centuries, old wood panels and carvings, line drawings, prints and paintings (none so bold as to compete with the tiny, exquisite bronzes) in a well-balanced, harmonious, eye-catching arrangement.

Although antique china, glass and silver might seem on the surface to be out of place in a strictly contemporary interior, they actually gain stature by being transposed in time. Against the flat planes and spare lines of today's architecture and furniture, the shapes, colors and patterns for which old Wedgwood, Baccarat and Georgian silver are prized emerge in a way they could never do in a period room. Simple Staffordshire china, glowing jewel-like in a strip-lighted niche, takes on a new quality in the sleekly contemporary dining room opposite, sheerly by virtue of the unusual setting.

Choosing objects for their spirit and shape rather than their intrinsic value is a characteristic of twentieth-century taste. In this context, folk art may be as highly esteemed as Fabergé, carnival glass as Lalique. Room dividers are popular as display cases for this kind of unpretentious col-

lection because the open shelves allow amusing or unusual forms to show up more clearly. A simple wood room divider between foyer and living room, above, was the excuse for a light-hearted assemblage of a traveler's acquisitions, ranging from an English Toby jug and old-fashioned soda syphon

to a decoy duck and an Indian elephant, gaily caparisoned with paint. As the shelves are adjustable, the arrangement can be changed when it begins to pall or if some new find is added.

A variation on this room divider is a series of glass shelves, open on one side and closed off on the other by a panel of opaque glass that fills in space between a hall and kitchen, above. The forms and colors of glass, pottery and sea shells are shown to advantage (and slightly protected from dust) but also more softly silhouetted by the effect of the light-filtering glass backing.

Avid collectors who accumulate more than their rooms can hold have evolved a new system for showing off their finds—rotation. What seems at first to be a neatly displayed collection, above, is actually a well-organized storage wall where inexpensive folk art, boxes and ceramics from Latin America and Japan are ranged ready for the choosing. The inside workings of the wall are shown opposite, where many of the objects have been

shifted from their storehouse to glass shelves arranged on standards from floor to ceiling. Purchased sheerly for pleasure, the gay, crude, simple objects, inconsequential in themselves, would look insignificant if alone or scattered at random. Only in a massed arrangement or interspersed, as they are here, with spools of colorful fibers (the owner-collector is a fabric designer who uses the tools of his trade as decoration) do they take on meaning.

Progress in America has become so accelerated that it has been said that many new buildings are outmoded before they are completed. Similarly, when the new cultural revolution broke, few houses could absorb the rising tide of books and the burgeoning paraphernalia of music.

DECORATING AROUND MUSIC AND BOOKS

JUST when music rooms and libraries had vanished from the blueprint (although provision might be made for that child of the century, the television room), America did a complete about-face and plunged into a major cultural renaissance. Contemporary houses, constructed without so much as a bookshelf (the lack of built-ins was one reason for the spurt of do-it-yourself carpentry during the postwar years), were suddenly found to be bursting at the seams with books, from the plebeian paperbacks to the more elegant breed of expensive gift books without which no Christmas-present list could exist. Music equipment expanded from the simple phonograph and radio to elaborate systems replete with stereo speakers and tape recorders, and not only the piano but even the home organ and player piano were heard throughout the land. Provision had to be made for both the sight and sound— or acoustical aspect—of music. The limited modern house, lacking the old spaciousness where there was always a room to spare, had to be painstakingly and adroitly planned if the more cerebral forms of home entertaining were to be dovetailed with activities already accommodated in the living room or family room. Something had to go, and it was usually the more expendable furniture. Rooms were pared down to the essentials, and where a large armoire or cabinet appeared it often turned out to be housing the music system. In the living room opposite, the space by the window wall which would once have held a conversation group is now devoted solely to showing off the classic beauty of a grand piano, raised on a platform and silhouetted against cove-lighted draperies like a piece of sculpture. This, plus the free-standing wall of books to the left of the piano and the display case for art at the opposite end of the room, is proof that the pleasures of the mind have as much influence on decoration today as the comforts of the body.

168

Despite the demise of the music room, the revival of music at home flourished with all the lively eighteenth-century spirit of participation. Friends formed string quartets and choral groups, families took up the guitar, folk singing and the home organ, a compact and mellifluous instrument so simplified and amplified through electronics that, as the makers boasted, even a child could play it. With the contours of console pianos and organs pared down and styled like traditional or modern furniture, the music area became an accepted part of many living rooms and family rooms. In the living room above, one end has been pre-empted as a music and book area. The level of the floor is slightly raised, like a modified concert platform, and a legless sofa grounded on it so that neither the sight nor the sound of the piano is blocked. The music area in the room opposite is a compact built-in wall, fully equipped with a small home organ, television and stereo system. Tuner, amplifier, turntable and twin speakers are unobtrusively fitted in the shelves among books and accessories.

As the quality and performance of music equipment steadily improved, it brought brand-new problems of room arrangement. If stereo was to be heard at its proper concert pitch, the floor plan had to be re-evaluated and the furniture regrouped. And, since true hi-fi buffs scorned the ready-made radio-phonograph combinations and preferred to put together their own systems, it was necessary to give the component parts some kind of unifying covering. One of the most practical solutions proved to be the built-in music center, where any components could be arranged to give best results and the sound projected into the middle of the room.

In the living room above, where the music center is fitted into a niche between fireplace and door, the turntable and tape recorder are sunk into a deep, wall-hung counter, the top screened by sliding panels, records are stored underneath and tuner and amplifier are at the left. When doors and panels are closed, the music wall merges into the

paneled background. A smaller, simpler music set-up (left) shares space with television and bar cabinets. The record player is built in below the counter top, behind pull-out doors, the speakers recessed at ceiling height. In the handsome and well-designed teak music center below, deep drawers file records and hold the tape recorder; radio and record player are within easy reach of the sofa, and the speakers are hidden behind an Oriental carved wood panel. Recessed doors pull out to cover the television set and music components so that the wall, when not in use, presents a smooth façade broken only by open shelves holding a few superb examples of Oriental and pre-Columbian art. This kind of custom-made center, both costly and static, nevertheless introduced the concept of music equipment as furniture. Instead of the unsightly cabinets of the past, music is now fitted into adaptable furniture—cocktail and end tables, desks and corner cupboards which conceal the mechanism and make placement simple.

THE MODERN LIBRARY
IN SMALL SPACE

NOTWITHSTANDING the prevalence of one-story houses, one-room apartments and the ubiquitous television set, the reading and ownership of books continue to increase. Although a fair proportion of the current spate of reading matter that overflows the stacks of bookstores and the stands in drugstores, air and rail terminals may be the expendable paperback of slaughter and seduction, there are still enough books of quality and merit being sold today to fill several million bookshelves. As only twelve percent of the houses built between 1949 and 1959 contained bookshelves and no new apartment house has been known to sully its virgin walls with them, the fact that people persist in buying and keeping books is the result of much determination and more ingenuity. Given the will, it is possible to find a way to have books in every room, including the kitchen and bathroom. Room-divider shelves and plug-in storage walls are easily installed in city apartments and rented houses, built-in shelves can be fitted into odd corners and niches such as the space between two windows in the apartment at the right—and enough shelves, scattered throughout the house, add up to a fair-sized library. Like art and music, books have become so familiar a part of the good life at home that a room would seem strangely barren without them, for the paintings we enjoy, the music we listen to and the books we read are the most direct expression of our personal taste and interests. Although few people today stock their shelves with the morocco-bound phalanxes of old, they may have their modern favorites rebound in leather. But most people prefer to leave books in their original covers and jackets, which have so improved in color and design that even a paper-bound volume of plays or essays can look like a work of art.

Today, books need no longer stand alone on shelves. Much of the fascination of the book wall opposite arises from the juxtaposition of books, varied in size, shape and binding or book jacket, with all kinds of other objects, ranging from records in brightly colored sleeves to antique glass and ceramics. The casual but cleverly composed arrangement is typical of the way books are now regarded and used, as an integral part of the decoration of the room. The bookshelves themselves could not be simpler. They are merely straight planks from the lumberyard, supported by wall strips and adjustable brackets and painted dark espresso brown to blend with the wall and throw the books and objects into relief. Any space, no matter how limited, is an opportunity for the book addict. In the living room above, an adroit variation on the stacks of public libraries fills in a narrow end wall without crowding floor space. Elevated on a small platform, a free-standing bookcase of three units topped with a pediment provides a tiny but adequate library-within-a-room.

Where the desire for a library exists, space can always be found, even in the most uncluttered contemporary apartment. The curving semicircular room-divider wall above and left, basically designed as a buffer zone between the foyer and living room, became a small but perfectly adequate library when it was lined with bookshelves, then carpeted and furnished to give the illusion of being a separate and secluded room. Library steps provide the boost required to reach the topmost bookshelves, and an open-arm chair can be drawn up to the table for quiet on-the-spot research.

Although plug-in pole systems and free-standing room dividers have made libraries independent of walls, the solid backing of a row of built-in bookshelves always makes a room seem more furnished. With little more than bookshelves and a table-desk, a corner of the living room above was converted into a self-contained library and home office. A fringed Spanish rug marks off the boundaries of the area and draws attention to the book corner. Clip-on students' lamps direct light downward onto reference works and pull-out shelves for heavy books while small sculptures, arranged on shelves shadow-box style to break the regularity of the

serried ranks of volumes, are silhouetted by fluorescent strip back lighting.

One of the most logical but often overlooked spots to assemble a library is a hallway, for most of them flaunt an inordinate amount of wasted wall space. Bookshelves running the length of the hallway opposite, from floor to ceiling, can clearly hold as many books as most families are likely to own in a lifetime. Upper hallways like this are favored because they are out of the mainstream of family traffic and also less likely to harbor dust, but if the books are precious enough to merit more protection, they may be shielded by glass doors.

In the 1950's, fireplaces and lighting, two of the most
traditionally hidebound elements of interiors, were freed
from the straitjacket of convention to take a big leap forward.
Radical new forms in hearths and hidden, versatile
sources of light did much to alter and advance decoration.

NEW SOURCES OF HEAT AND LIGHT

I F FORM follows function, as Mies van der Rohe would have us believe, then fireplaces and lighting have been laggards for decades. Until fairly recently, the family hearth had altered hardly a whit from the heat-giving source of our ancestors—a fire box recessed in the wall and ventilated by a flue and a chimney. Although the primary function of the fireplace, to give out warmth, had been long superseded by the more efficient heating system and was now mainly retained for the sensuous pleasure of flames and firelight, it still kept its archaic form. The same was true of lighting. The electric table lamp is merely an extension of the rush taper, candle and oil lamp; the lighting fixture derives from the wall sconce, chandelier and gas jet. Yet in an age when practically every element pertaining to the decoration of houses was being re-evaluated or redesigned, the fireplaces and lighting to be found in the majority of houses and apartments were completely outmoded. The improvements that eventually came about in the fifties and sixties arose directly from the discoveries and influence of contemporary architecture. Built-in over-all illumination by means of recessed ceiling spotlights, cornice and soffit lighting and luminous walls and ceilings, first introduced in public buildings, soon appeared on the domestic scene. In the more design-conscious new houses, fireplaces were looked on as an integral part of the architecture. The shape and materials of the fireplace were chosen to reflect and enhance the nature of the room, and the hearth was frequently raised or cantilevered to form a wide shelf for seating or the display of objects. In the two-story living room opposite, the fireplace and elevated hearth are of filled and polished travertine, a structural material widely used in modern architecture. Walnut fretwork grilles, rather than solid walls, flank the fireplace, partially screening a ramp leading to a gallery and giving a sense of see-through dimension and lightness to the room's fourth face.

When the architects took over, the design of fireplaces became much more daring. No longer were they rigidly confined to a wall; instead, they moved out into the room, often taking up a central position. Pure form was emphasized, rather than the fussy detail of old, and the results were frequently both functional and as striking as sculpture. As the fireplace by nature of its size was one of the most dominant elements in the room, impossible to overlook, the dramatic spareness of its shape was played up as a focal point. In the living room opposite, a fireplace-in-the-round soars like a structural column, silhouetted against the window wall. Sunk in a tiled pit and hedged on three sides by a seating platform, the hearth has the lure of a campfire, and can in fact, with the screens around the brazier-like firebox drawn back, be used for grilling.

The shaped metal chimney at the right, rather like an overgrown stovepipe with a sculptured base, is another form of fireplace that sprang from an architect's drawing board. Prefabricated and easy to install, it can be built into a new house or added to an old one, provided there is a flue.

Free-standing stoves with fanciful shapes (the popular acorn stove might have been dreamed up by Disney) represent one of the simplest and least expensive ways to add a fireplace to a room that lacks one. Although these stoves are not especially commanding, they can be given more prominence and importance by the kind of clever decorating trick shown at the right. Here a black iron stove is mounted on a platform in the center of the room and screened on two sides with heat-reflecting panels of opaque glass set in aluminum frames and angled to leave space for plants. Not only new but also old stoves are having a vogue at present, notably the elegant Austrian porcelain stove (more for its beauty than its ability to radiate heat) and that all-time favorite, the stalwart Franklin stove.

Once it was established that the fireplace of today had little or nothing in common with the fireplace of the past, it came to be regarded in a new light, as an integral and, above all, functional part of the room scheme. Fireplaces took on the aspect of sculpture or furniture, the attributes of room dividers. No conventional fireplace would have appeared in the guise above, as the central partner in a triumvirate of wall-recessed television, hearth and hi-fi, styled like a cabinet, that fits neatly into the long wall at one end of the living room as a focal point for the seating group. The fireplace-entertainment center is carefully designed to conform to the scale and contours of the room and the furniture. When the television set and music system are not in operation, tambour doors slide over, blending the façade with the wall. A single oil painting, deliberately hung off-center, breaks the regularity of the line.

In the cathedral living room opposite, the hearth is again subordinated to the guiding concept of function, for here the chimney forms an architectural divider between living and dining areas. This purpose is underlined by a narrow table that, following the shape of the fireplace, holds magazines and flowers on one side and acts as an end table on the other. The hearth itself, open on either side, and graceful electrified chandeliers, suspended and swaying like mobiles, are all that relieve the height and severity of the two-story fireplace wall.

As fireplaces changed over from traditional to contemporary forms, the elaborate overmantel and mantelshelf of old were pared away, leaving little more than a plain wall or panel of stone, brick, wood, marble or plaster to enclose and delineate the fireplace and hearth—the latter also frequently refined out of existence. An example of this understated treatment is shown in the penthouse living room opposite, where a four-square, marble-faced column set into the center of a glass window wall contains the fireplace and cantilevered hearth, an arrangement that permits furniture to be grouped on all three sides. In an equally modern metamorphosis, the fireplace in the room above is set behind a stark and unadorned concrete slab that forms part of a divider wall between the foyer and the living areas. The hearth, in this case at floor level, is not emphasized at all. In both rooms, the contemporary character of the fireplaces is matched by the lighting. Floor and table lamps have been forgone in favor of built-in lighting beamed from the ceiling and, in the case of the living room above, a pair of airy Japanese paper lanterns silhouetted against the window wall.

THE SWITCH TO
BUILT-IN LIGHTING

No one has shed a tear over the demise of that stereotype of bad decorating, the lamp in the picture window. One of the more welcome decorating freedoms, won within this generation, is freedom from the tyranny of table and floor lamps, inflexibly tied to cords and outlets. The emergence of built-in lighting, which broke the stranglehold and virtually eliminated the role of lamps, has made an invaluable contribution to the cause of contemporary decoration. For built-in lighting has the protean ability to project any form of illumination, from the general to the specific, that might be needed in a room. Spotlights set in coves or soffits can be directed up or down to reflect light softly from ceiling, walls or draperies. They can be recessed in the ceiling, clipped to a pole or beam and trained on a single part of the room or point of the decoration. With the addition of a dimmer system, a turn of the knob modulates the intensity of light by increasing or decreasing the voltage.

The nuances of built-in lighting are especially welcome in large open-plan living rooms, like the one at the right, where half-a-dozen different activities may be going on at once. Here the strong daylight that floods through the glass walls can be equaled at night by cove lighting recessed in an inverted trough over the music and storage wall, supplemented by decorative hanging fixtures strategically placed over the dining table and near the sofa. Recessed downlights in the ceiling areas near the windows offset the blankness of uncurtained glass after nightfall. Table and floor lamps are significantly absent, for one of the main tenets of modern lighting philosophy is that wherever possible the viewer should only be conscious of light and never of the source of light, which is either completely hidden or kept well above eye level.

When lighting is skillfully built in, it does much more than merely illuminate. Like any other facet of interior decoration, lighting can abet architecture or, if necessary, compensate for structural drawbacks. The long lighting trough that was designed to fit neatly into an awkward niche in the wall of the foyer above is primarily a means of lighting an area without windows. Striplights in the trough, diffused and subdued by glass panels, cast light directly on the desk and on the narrow carving set in the wall niche. However, by bridging the gap from wall to wall, the lighting fixture coor-

dinates the small cut-up space and sets it off visually from the adjoining living room. Another form of concealed lighting that helps to stress one particular area is shown in the family room above, where a lowered ceiling of narrow wood slats with fluorescent strips behind is suspended like a canopy over a raised concert platform. Downlighting is balanced by lights set into panels in the wall and intensified by glass shelves, making the entire end of the room glow like a stage and giving both musicians and listeners excellent visibility when lights in the room are turned low during a performance.

One of the particular properties of good lighting is the power to suggest not only the mood but also the measure of a room. Small pools of light dotted at random can make a room seem shrunken and cramped, whereas large areas of softly diffused light give a sense of spaciousness. The same holds true outdoors; the world looks very different on sunlit and dark days. Emulating the oldest light source of all, indoor lighting derives many ideas from daylight and sunlight (the pinpoint spot that picks out the sparkle of crystal or the patina of gold is just another kind of sunbeam, with the same capacity to enhance a glittering object).

The recessed downlights over the windows in the room below and the soffit lighting over the curtained window wall opposite take advantage of the

reflective values of white walls and draperies to give the effect of the gentle over-all light of day. The luminous ceiling and wall, where fluorescent strips or floodlights are set behind panels of opaque translucent plastic or glass, represent other successful attempts to copy nature. This popular form of lighting, chiefly seen in kitchens, bathrooms or small enclosed areas such as foyers or dressing rooms, is the forerunner of electroluminescence, a new concept in which the wall or ceiling will actually be the light source, a sandwich-like panel coated to conduct electricity and glow with light. This experiment in lighting has so far been confined, on the domestic level, to small nightlights that plug into baseboard outlets, but it promises to open up a wide new horizon for interior lighting.

Interior decoration soon outgrew the timid early stages when rooms were safely pegged to a single look, color scheme or period of design. Mixtures of unmatched furniture and accessories became not only permissible but a positive statement of personal taste in the face of the rubber-stamp conformity of mass-produced architecture.

FINESSE WITH FURNITURE

To EVOLVE a distinct decorating style that holds true for a whole country demands will, skill and wherewithal, all of which exist in America today on an unprecedented scale. Two decades of experiment have brought us maturity of taste and judgment and the ability to be original. Copy-cat decorating that follows the dictates of the trend-setting few is out, so are all-of-a-piece rooms as impersonal as a store display. With good design spreading through mass production to every price level, with the international influence of an influx of goods from all over the world, and with furniture manufacturers abandoning their one-style lines in favor of the diversified group, America resembles a vast bazaar, where the freedom of choice is staggering. From all of this largesse has come a significant and far-reaching development in decoration called, for want of a more euphonious name, mixing. Period furniture is mixed with contemporary, antique accessories are ranged on modern storage walls, in a completely uninhibited and personal way. Revivals of the best in America's historic furniture—Shaker, Mission and Colonial—mingle with exciting sculptural shapes from contemporary designers, with European antiques and with accessories culled from every corner of the globe. In a brilliant exposition of the art of mixing, contemporary American upholstered furniture is played off, in the room opposite, against the curving contours of a Louis XV open-arm chair, painted vivid green, a red-upholstered wing chair and a Queen Anne chair with a dark wood frame. Two of the tables in the room, a glass-and-iron coffee table and red-lacquered table desk, are modern, but the end tables, a bouillotte and a Chinese ceramic garden stool, owe their graceful lines to two of the great French and Oriental design periods. Accessories run the gamut from an ancient T'ang horse to a crystal cigarette cup in the modern Scandinavian manner. Unexpected in a room with a preponderance of traditional furniture, the dark walls and bleached wood floor have the studied effect of uniting and calming down the lively hodgepodge of colors, shapes and styles.

The successful crossing of centuries calls for an appreciation of balance, form and harmony, an eye for compatible shapes and a sense of lightness that brings a room to life by introducing, as a final note, a totally unorthodox touch. In the room opposite, where one of the most classic of straight-lined contemporary sofas is teamed with a rush-seated Louis XVI armchair, a small French Empire chest, an Oriental rug and a modern glass-and-metal table akin to the designs of the Directoire period, the surprise is the juxtaposition of two utterly dissimilar paintings—a glowing sixteenth-century oil on a saffron wall and an example of the current white-on-white school on a white wall. In the sitting room above, proof that a beautiful antique stands out better in a modern setting than in a traditional one, striped wallpaper, a dark green rug and sofas slip-covered in a flower print point up the size and elaborate detail of a Chippendale secretary and the curves of a Queen Anne chair. The punch line is the presence, in a room that verges on the formal, of a pair of functional brass pole lights.

by luxurious upholstery that, like flesh over bare bones, pads without disguising the underlying structure. A perfect example is the lounge chair and ottoman designed by Eero Saarinen in 1946, in the room above. The plastic shell, covered with foam rubber and taut upholstery and resting lightly on a slender metal frame, qualifies on every count of function, form and aesthetics.

Many of the shapes seen in present-day furniture have their roots in industry. Swivel chairs and mushroom tables, stacking chairs and chests were originally designed for commercial and industrial use; the bucket seat of automobiles and airplanes was the predecessor of the famous Eames plastic shell chair. The steel cage chairs opposite indicate the direction in which furniture design is moving. Such experiments are leading toward new applications of the principles of suspension to achieve a space-saving see-through quality and a hitherto unparalleled lightness and "give."

206

PRODUCT OF THE CENTURY – THE NEW WAVE
IN FURNITURE WOODS AND FINISHES

DESPITE the material changes wrought in furniture by steel and plastics, wood has shown its strength by adapting in this century, as it has done in the past, to the tenor of the times, an attribute that has made it so invaluable a part of the interior decorating of every era. The history of furniture can almost be traced through the ways in which wood was used. In the early days, when great oak forests stretched across Europe, this was the favored material for the Gothic, Tudor and early Renaissance styles, and the toughness and resistance of the wood was mainly responsible for the crudeness and heaviness of the carving on chairs, tables and chests. By the seventeenth century, with the forests depleted, oak was largely displaced by walnut, and in the eighteenth century, when cabinetwork was at its zenith, mahogany was the chosen wood because it was easy to work and took a beautiful satiny finish.

In this generation, we have seen a vogue for the blond birchwood and korina and the bleached finishes that spelled Swedish Modern, and for teak, an Oriental wood little known in other periods and now overwhelmingly identified with contemporary furniture, especially the Scandinavian. But undoubtedly the greatest advance in furniture design of the present generation has been the development of bent and molded plywood and the laminated woods. Plywood, whether molded into original, figure-conforming shapes such as the chair that gained Charles Eames the Museum of Modern Art furniture award for design in 1946, or applied to a flat surface in the form of veneer, has virtually revolutionized furniture construction. Apart from the fact that it is stronger, lighter and infinitely less expensive than solid wood of the same thickness, plywood has great flexibility and, when bonded to a hard core, incredible staying power, since the construction insures that it will not warp under pressure or atmospheric changes. In the room opposite, which might be said to capsule the progress of wood down the ages, the apparently authentic beams and paneling are teak plywood. The chest and chair in front of the paneling are oak, heavily carved in the Renaissance style, the Louis XVI chair behind the lacquered table-desk is carved mahogany with a bleached finish and the Régence chair in the foreground is fruitwood. The tones, textures and grains of wood supply all the decorative interest in the room.

The unfamiliar light tone of the mahogany chair points up another far-reaching development in furniture today, the refinement of wood finishes. The new finishes can simulate, in reproductions, the handwork of antiques; they can make one wood look like another (birch is often stained and finished to imitate such expensive cabinet woods as walnut and mahogany); they can lighten the traditionally dark woods. This has resulted in a revival of mahogany, no longer in the characteristic red-browns of the Georgian, French Empire and American Federal periods, but in a paler brown better suited to contemporary rooms. The improvements in finishes and veneers have led to a small but significant trend to a greater degree of ornamentation in furniture, either through the use of exotic wood veneers, such as rosewood and paldao, or through decorative inlays of ebony, zebrawood and myrtle burl, that to some extent replace the cabinetwork of the past and the hand detailing that modern machine construction, despite its many advantages, has never been able to match.

All furniture owes something to the past, for, as Sir Winston Churchill
once remarked, "Without tradition, design is a flock of sheep
without a shepherd." The furniture of today can trace its roots back
as far as the Greco-Roman era, and its great ancestors
are to be found in every major period of design innovation and experiment.

FURNITURE FAMILY TREE

THE UNDERLYING relationship that makes an eighteenth-century sofa perfectly at home with a nineteenth-century bentwood rocker and a twentieth-century steel-and-glass coffee table may not be apparent at first glance. It becomes more easily perceptible and understandable once you appreciate the characteristics of the design periods and styles of the past. The furniture family tree evolved in a gradual progression that might see in one century a great leap forward in design and in another a noticeable digression and preoccupation with artifice and ornamentation. Some styles have not only endured but are widely used, both as antiques and in reproductions, for contemporary room settings where the current vogue for mixing is in evidence. Others look right only in museums or in rigidly interpreted period rooms with their own kind. Wherein lies the difference between a period and a style? This is hard to pinpoint, but it is a little like the branches of a family within a given generation. Generally speaking, styles occurred in a distinct design period and were often named for their originators (Adam, Chippendale, Duncan Phyfe) or for a certain reign within that period (Queen Anne, Directoire). During the eighteenth century alone, the heyday of design, widely divergent styles flourished. They ran the gamut from classical revivals inspired by the excavations of Pompeii and Herculaneum through rococo interpretations of natural motifs and baroque echoes of the Renaissance to Oriental imports and Western translations from the Chinese. For the most part, styles overlapped and merged. Some were influenced by the mode prevailing in another country, while others were purely native and arose from the needs and taste of the day. Those that have withstood the test of time have remained popular, while others that were fads in their day are now either dead or revived as curiosities. That is true of this century, where amid a flood of furniture only a few classics, rising head and shoulders above the others, can be said to represent contemporary design.

Chinese

Classical

Gothic

Queen Anne

French Régence

Renaissance

Louis Quatorze

William and Mary

Louis Quinze

Chippendale

Early American

Late American

French Provincial

Italian Provincial

Louis Seize

Hepplewhite

Adam

Sheraton

Directoire

English Regency

Biedermeier

French Empire

Federal

Duncan Phyfe

Victorian

Shaker

Mission

Art Nouveau

Twentieth Century

CLASSICAL

The ancient Greek and Roman furniture from which so much later design stemmed was one with the architecture of the times, where proportion and symmetry were in perfect balance. The Greek klismos, a side chair, inspired a similar style in French Directoire, English Regency and the contemporary furniture of the twentieth century. The folding stool, borrowed from Egypt, developed into the Roman curule with curved X-form legs, and is now a classic of contemporary design. The kline, or couch, used by both the Greeks and the Romans for reclined dining and sleeping, was the inspiration for the elegant Récamier chaise longue, while the Greek and Roman tripod tables with animal forms for legs reappeared cast in bronze, as were many of the originals. The Roman throne chair, a derivation from the Greek, cropped up again during the Renaissance and was a favorite chair style of the French Empire. The eighteenth-century excavations of the ancient cities of Pompeii and Herculaneum, buried in A.D. 79 by an eruption of Mount Vesuvius, unearthed furniture which was copied exactly or adapted into the classic styles of Adam, Louis XVI and French Empire.

CHINESE

The second great style influence on furniture design in the eighteenth and ensuing centuries was the Orient. The cabriole leg, introduced in English Queen Anne and French Louis XV furniture, was undoubtedly inspired by a similar Chinese design; and the use of lacquer as a finishing material, developed by Queen Anne cabinetmakers and continued in the great chinoiserie movement of Louis XV's reign, derived directly from Chinese lacquered pieces. Chinese lattice designs caught the fancy of Chippendale, resulting in a whole school of Chinese Chippendale furniture. Oriental woods —teak, sandalwood and bamboo—were the rage in Regency England. Even the Victorians, in their endless search for the novel, turned out clumsy and ornate pieces in the Chinese style. So-called "Chinese Modern," the hit of the 1930's and 1940's, was based on Chinese household furniture. Today, many contemporary designs reflect the best characteristics of Chinese design: simplicity of line and construction, minimum ornamentation, use of beautiful woods and lacquered surfaces.

Roman stone throne chair,
1st century A.D.

Greco-Roman bronze curule, 100 B.C.

Greek lectus, 5th century B.C.

Lohan armchair with curved back rail

Wooden K'ang day bed with swastika back

K'ang table with cabriole leg

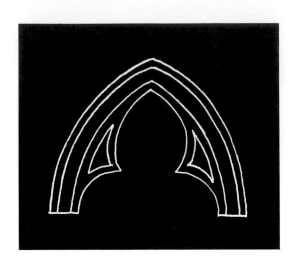

GOTHIC

1100–1500

The paragon of style during this period of the Middle Ages was the Church, because the Church was the only stable factor. The architecture of the great Gothic cathedrals with their pointed arches, buttresses and pillars decorated with molding and unique details was the obvious inspiration for furniture, at however great a remove. Moreover, since Europe was at this time continually at war, it was desirable that household effects should be mobile. Chests and coffers were the main furniture. Folding chairs were carried for lords and ladies, throne chairs for court sessions. In lieu of tables, boards were set on trestles. The luxury of sleeping in privacy and warmth depended on an enclosure that was easily transportable, consisting of framework, curtains, canopy and bedding. This remained popular until rooms became small enough to afford equivalent comforts. Today, Gothic furniture survives in modern versions of the four-poster bed and joint stools and coffers now pressed into service as end tables or for decorative storage.

Distinguishing features. All furniture was oak, unpolished and carved with a heavy hand. Panels in chests were decorated with linen-fold or tracery carving or painted designs based on floral or grotesque animal or human forms, humorously drawn.

214

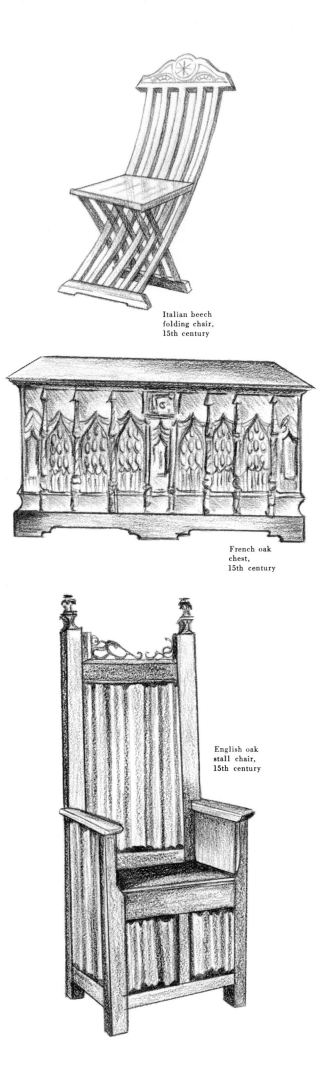

Italian beech
folding chair,
15th century

French oak
chest,
15th century

English oak
stall chair,
15th century

Flemish walnut chair, 17th century

RENAISSANCE   1500–1700

In reaction to Gothic, a style was literally reborn that reclaimed the classic heritage of Greece and Rome. In Italy, where the movement had its roots, an architectural feeling predominated in furniture. Later pieces, embellished in line and ornamentation, represent the style as we know it today. As political changes wrought economic improvements during this period, a more comfortable and settled home life took shape, and furniture became essential and developed new forms. Almost all Renaissance pieces, however rudimentary in form and stature, are recognizable ancestors of present-day furniture.

Distinguishing features. In France, the scale of the later Italian Renaissance pieces was resolved to livable proportions, but carving was elaborated. In Spain, where the Moorish influence was strong, Eastern motifs were introduced in inlays and ornate metal mounts and brass studdings. In Flanders, the interpretation resulted in heavy, square and solid proportions with carving often abandoned for turning. In Tudor England, the carving and decoration were more elaborate, the shapes stiff, straight and massive. Oak and walnut were the prevailing woods in all countries.

French walnut draw-top table, late 16th century

English oak court cupboard, early 17th century

LOUIS QUATORZE   1643–1715

A baroque style of furniture developed during the reign of Louis XIV, characterized by sumptuous scale and symmetry, and masculine despite its lavish ornamentation. Carving was rich and, had it not been confined to the prevailing straight line, might have been considered indiscriminate. The famous cabinetmaker, Boulle, perfected intricate marquetry of tortoise shell, brass, ivory, bone and mother-of-pearl. Exceptional gilding further enhanced the more massive pieces. The heavy tables were so immobile that console tables were developed. In seating pieces, the "confessional," the first of the fully upholstered bergères and sofas, appeared. Generally speaking, the style and size of Louis XIV is not appropriate to today's houses. However, country pieces of this period are currently enjoying a revival.

Distinguishing features. Straight lines, restrained curves, plentiful carving. Plain woods were given more magnificence by the decorative application of marquetry panels, gilding and vernis Martin.

WILLIAM AND MARY
1689–1702

The names of Mary Stuart and her Dutch husband William III, who popularized the Dutch idea of comfort, have become synonymous with a style and period of furniture made, for the first time, for the public. Cabinetmakers from Flanders, Holland and France were influenced by the rich baroque style of Louis XIV, while England's Christopher Wren worked in the more chaste Italian image. The melding of the two schools produced furniture that was no longer so grand. As rooms became smaller and more intimate, furnishings adopted a lighter, simpler scale and style in keeping with the new domesticity. Today, period pieces of this style are hard to come by, but many nineteenth-century copies are available.

Distinguishing features. Chunky but small-scale; legs turned and braced with serpentine stretchers; the Dutch club foot and scroll leg that forecast the Queen Anne cabriole leg; chairs padded and often covered with needle-point. Walnut replaced English oak; veneering and marquetry of exotic woods, lacquer and japanning became popular.

Natural oak console table

Boulle commode

Walnut open-arm chair

Walnut lowboy

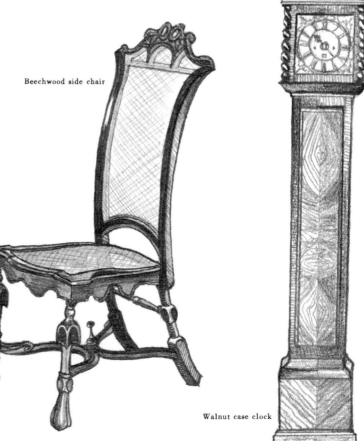

Beechwood side chair

Walnut case clock

QUEEN ANNE 1702–1715

The reign of Queen Anne inspired both a style and a period of furniture easily recognized by the cabriole leg and undulating lines. Improved cabinetry techniques made stretchers unnecessary. Catering to comfort, furniture makers of the period introduced upholstery in the overstuffed manner, and chair backs with a single curved splat, fiddle- or vase-shaped and spooned to fit the back. Some innovations were stimulated by such social amenities as tea drinking, responsible for the small tea table, and the craze for collecting china, which brought into being the glass-doored closet. Others, equally tailored to the times, were highboys, the forerunners of vertical storage pieces, Windsor and banister back chairs. In comfort, scale and simplicity, Queen Anne furniture is admirably capable of combining with modern furniture.

Distinguishing features. Simplicity of line, absence of flamboyant decoration. Walnut was the favorite surface, often lacquered or gilded, with some marquetry. Carving took the form of the scallop shell, acanthus leaf, broken and C-curve.

Chinese lacquer secretary

Cherry armchair, scrolled splat back

Walnut chaise longue

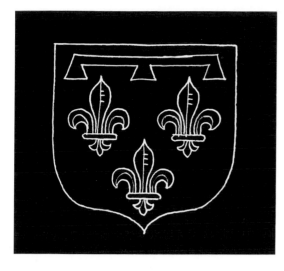

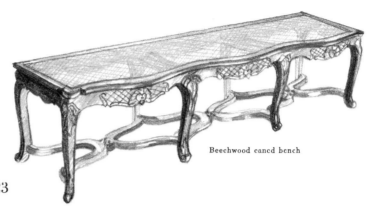

Beechwood caned bench

FRENCH RÉGENCE 1715–1723

When France was under the regency of Philippe, Duc d'Orléans, furniture was in a transitional style which bridged the massive grandeur of Louis XIV and the more feminine persuasion of Louis XV. Rococo ornamentation was introduced, and many new pieces needed for personal storage emerged in France during this time, including the commode, the secrétaire and the chiffonier.

Distinguishing features. Cabriole leg with doe foot, stretchered chairs. Carved ornamentation, profuse though delicate in execution, is distinguished from that of Louis XV because it is clearly confined within architectural outlines.

Walnut bergère

Rosewood veneer commode

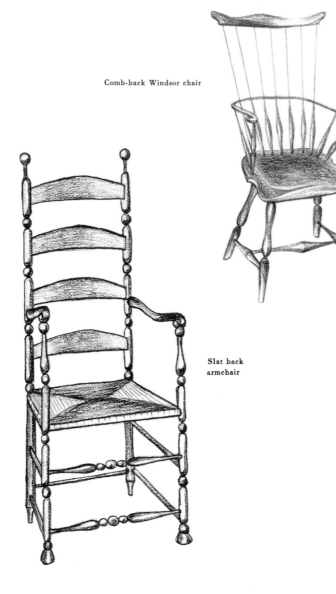

Comb-back Windsor chair

Slat back
armchair

Butterfly table

AMERICAN COLONIAL

Furniture produced in America before the Revolution may be roughly divided into two categories, Early and Late Colonial. In the early days, furniture reflected the styles of the day in England. New England settlers adapted Jacobean and Elizabethan designs, in crude but serviceable versions and woods like pine, oak and maple. For the most part, pieces were unfinished and allowed to acquire color, depth and patina through years of use and natural darkening. Need, rather than fashion, prescribed the types of furniture made at the time: unadorned chests and cupboards for storage; simple trestle and gate-leg tables; banister and ladder back chairs and rockers with solid wood, rush or leather seats. In Pennsylvania, German and Swiss colonists produced what we now call Pennsylvania Dutch (from *Deutsch*), with strong Tyrolean influences in brightly painted and decorated pieces. The kas, or bride's dower chest, was perhaps the most famous contribution. In California and the Southwest, the Spanish left their mark in Mission and Ranch styles. As the colonies prospered in the

Wing chair with Queen Anne leg

Goddard block-front chest

Early, 1620–1670   Late, 1700–1790

eighteenth century, more craftsmen arrived from England, bringing with them later styles which were promptly copied locally but simplified and changed in proportion and scale to suit American tastes and houses. By 1750, distinct American styles of furniture were being made in walnut and mahogany in Boston, Newport, New York and Philadelphia. American Colonial is by far the most popular style of furniture reproduced here, and original pieces are the most sought after.

Distinguishing features. Early legs were square and rough-hewn; later ones have simple turnings. The back legs of American Queen Anne chairs are straighter than those of the English, and American Chippendale chairs have higher backs and lack the ornate carving of the originals. Typical American pieces: the butterfly table; the Windsor chair in all its local variations; writing chairs with palettes attached; rocking chairs; ladder back chairs; beds with short posts and with four posts crowned by finials; block-front chests and secretaries made by Goddard and Townsend.

Curly maple highboy

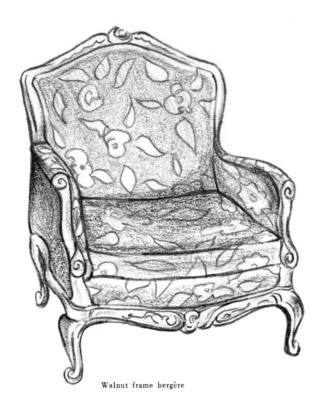

Walnut frame bergère

LOUIS QUINZE 1715–1774

Considered by many to be the ultimate in decorative furniture, the rococo style that emerged during the reign of Louis XV is essentially feminine in character. Symmetry was avoided, and every possible device was employed to detour the straight

Gothic style side chair

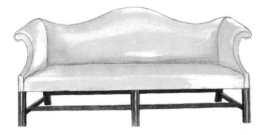

Camel-back sofa with mahogany frame

CHIPPENDALE 1740–1779

Developed by the master cabinetmaker and designer Thomas Chippendale, this is perhaps the most outstanding of the Georgian styles. Chippendale derived his inspiration from preceding English, French, and Chinese styles. The most

Lacquer bureau plat

Inlaid serpentine front commode

line into a soft curve. Comfort was emphasized, although artfully disguised, in chairs, sofas and chaise longues shaped to the human frame and often upholstered with loose down cushions. Commodes assumed many forms—bombé fronts and sides, slant fronts on desks. Every variety of table shared a common characteristic, the cabriole leg. *Distinguishing features.* Soft flowing lines, dainty

naturalistic ornamentation, the cabriole leg. Mahogany, native fruitwoods, walnut with veneers of the more exotic rosewood, satinwood, amaranth and tulip. An intrinsic part of the design was the decoration: marquetry, painting, lacquering and gilding, metal appliqués (on modest pieces, the bronzes were functional handles, locks and key escutcheons, feet), marble and other stones for tops.

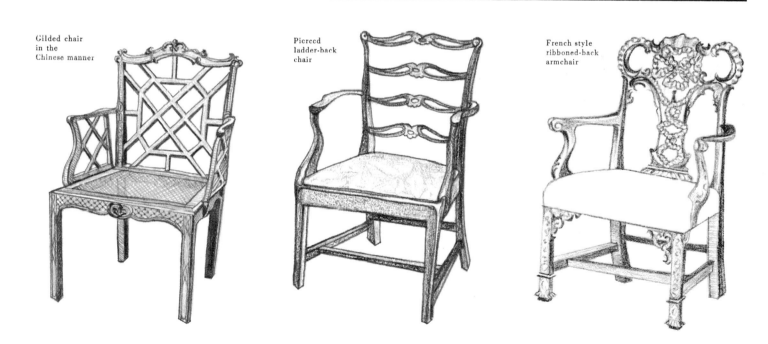

Gilded chair in the Chinese manner

Pierced ladder-back chair

French style ribboned-back armchair

reproduced of all English furniture, Chippendale has been and still is the most popular here.
Distinguishing features. In the early pieces, cabriole legs, claw-and-ball feet, heavy carved decoration and similar devices common to early eighteenth-century furniture. Later pieces, much more beautiful, have straight legs, pierced splats on chairs,

delicate carving in ribbons and scrolls, heavier carving in shells, acanthus leaves and dolphins, and fretwork (a characteristic of what is known as Chinese Chippendale). Almost all pieces of furniture were mahogany. Some were lacquered or gilded, occasionally veneered, but never inlaid, painted or with applied ornamentation.

223

FRENCH PROVINCIAL

1650–1900

French Provincial is not a period of design but a conglomeration of styles developed by the provincial craftsmen of France, mostly translations in simpler terms and materials of the Parisian court styles. The most familiar are those based on Louis XV and Louis XVI. Easily identified with French Provincial are types of furniture like the buffet, cupboard and armoire with the simple curve, and the more specialized lit clos, or built-in bed, the panetière, or breadbox, and rush-seated chairs. Today, eighteenth-century French Provincial is the most duplicated and offers the widest variety of pieces.

Distinguishing features. Woods of the provinces —walnut and fruitwoods—polished steel hardware in Lorraine; oak with brass fittings in Normandy; chestnut with copper in Provence. Decoration was limited to simple but well-executed carving, painted designs and handsome hinges and handles.

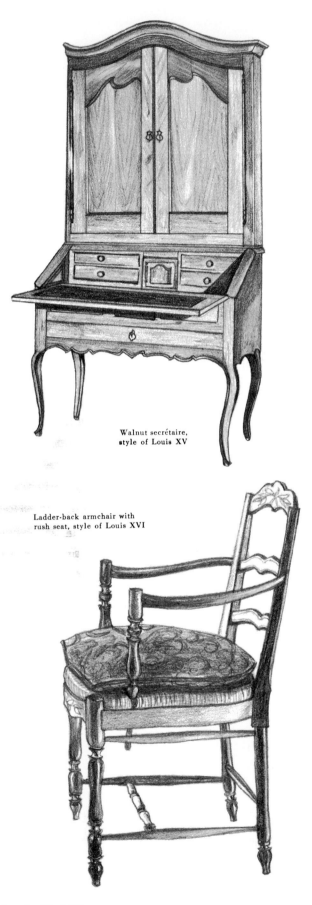

Walnut secrétaire,
style of Louis XV

Ladder-back armchair with
rush seat, style of Louis XVI

Cherry commode, style of Louis XV

Carved and gilded wood-frame settee

ADAM 1760–1800

Named for Robert, James and William Adam, architects who also designed furniture to fit the superb houses they built, this style belongs to the late Georgian period of eighteenth-century England. The designs of the Brothers Adam, based on Roman, Pompeian and French styles, were characterized by delicacy, restraint and classic simplicity. They favored mahogany and satinwood and motifs that ran the gamut from classical acanthus, pineapple, disks, ovals and floral swags to animal heads and human figures. Although Adam furniture has innate charm and beauty it lacks warmth and comfort, and is not especially suited to contemporary rooms.

Distinguishing features. Straight lines; tapering legs; low-relief carving on flat surfaces decorated with painting and gilding; inlays; carved moldings.

Shield back armchair

Serving table, wine cooler, pedestals with urn knife boxes

LOUIS SEIZE 1774–1793

The curve went into eclipse during the reign of Louis XVI, when a reaction to the frills of Louis XV inspired a return to the classic style. French cabinetmakers, like the Brothers Adam in England, were affected by the discoveries of Pompeii and Herculaneum and returned to ancient architectural forms. Although the actual pieces of furniture estab-

Oval-back side chair

Acajou commode with bronze-filled fluting

ITALIAN PROVINCIAL
1700–1850

Loosely applied to furniture made by the craftsmen of the Italian provinces in the eighteenth and early nineteenth centuries, this term embraces many styles that developed in Italy in much the same way as in France. Elaborate designs of Rome, Florence, Venice and Milan were simplified. Today, many reproductions have improved on the originals in scale, although the term has come to cover anything "Mediterranean" that is basically

lished under Louis Quinze continued, a few new shapes appeared, notably the curule bench, the roll-back sofa and glazed display cabinets known as vitrines. Not as universally appealing as Louis XV, Louis XVI is nevertheless easy to live with today because of its simplicity and restraint. *Distinguishing features.* Straight lines and rectangular planes with embellishments; tapered legs emphasized by fluting and grooving; flat panels enhanced by exquisite moldings. Classic ornamentation: laurel, egg and dart, palm leaves, fretwork rinceaux and ribbons. From Greco-Roman sources: swans, urns, wreaths, festoons, bound arrows, fanciful animals. Mahogany was the dominant wood but ebony, rosewood, tulip and others were combined in marquetry. Black and gold lacquer, gray-white to gray-green painted finishes and insets of Sèvres china were much admired.

Gilded bergère

Square-back fauteuil

Armchair in the Directoire manner

Side chair in the Queen Anne manner

straight rather than curved like French Provincial. *Distinguishing features.* Early pieces were strongly influenced by the baroque, large and bulky in scale but devoid of lavish decoration; later pieces reveal the neoclassical influence of the current French styles but have much more rusticity. More painted finishes are to be found in Italian Provincial, possibly because the cabinetmakers wished to disguise inferior woods or because of the Italian flair for decoration, especially evident in *arte pòvera,* painted paper imitations of carving.

HEPPLEWHITE c. 1770–1786

Cabinetmaker George Hepplewhite was responsible for a graceful but substantial style of English furniture inspired in part by French design of the Louis XVI period. Credited as the father of the modern sideboard, Hepplewhite favored serpentine fronts, six legs and concave corners that distinguish his pieces from the convex models of Sheraton. Today, Hepplewhite furniture enjoys a place primarily in dining rooms and as accents in other rooms.

Distinguishing features. Slender, fluted legs, spade feet; chairs with low backs; preponderance of curves; carving employed sparingly and generally classical, with the exception of the Prince of Wales' feathers introduced as a motif. Mahogany was the favorite wood, and embellishment usually took the form of beautiful veneers or painted scenes.

Satinwood breakfront bookcase

Feather back side chair

Show-wood frame sofa

228

SHERATON

1790–1805

This style of the late Georgian period took its name from Thomas Sheraton, author of *The Cabinet-maker and Upholsterer's Drawing Book*, a compendium of designs of the period. Sheraton's book assembled all the known available designs of the time, which eventually were mistakenly attributed to him. Many pieces, then dubbed "harlequin furniture," were early versions of what we now call dual-purpose furniture, and are equally versatile in today's homes. His later work, based on French Directoire and Empire, was not equal in caliber to the earlier designs.

Distinguishing features. Straight, classic lines in the manner of Hepplewhite and Adam, delicate and graceful, with the simplest ornamentation.

Leather-topped mahogany library table

Satinwood Pembroke table with inlays

Secretary with Gothic tracery

Rosewood credenza with brass mounts, and beech armchair, style of Louis XVI

ENGLISH REGENCY 1795–1820

A style that spanned the years of the Late Georgian era when George IV was Prince Regent and continued in favor to the end of his reign, best exemplified by the Brighton Pavilion. Not to be confused with French Régence, English Regency furniture was strongly influenced by the earlier French Directoire and Empire, with certain distinctive Egyptian and Chinese motifs, notably bamboo trimming and cane seats and backs. Simpler in line and smaller in scale than Chippendale, this furniture conveys a special intimate quality and to this day enjoys a well-deserved if limited popularity. Some smaller pieces are extremely witty and

Inlaid marble table with gilt, bronze and mahogany base

DIRECTOIRE 1795–1803

All signs of royal and aristocratic influences were eliminated during the Directory and Consulate of France, between the fall of Robespierre and the rise of Napoleon. The result was a simple and direct style of furniture with a dignity and stature of its own. Its charm prevails today in antiques and reproductions of such enduring designs as the Récamier chaise, the folding campaign chair.

Distinguishing features. Straight lines; judicious use of classic curves; motifs derived from the antique, like swans, stars and lyres, and French Revolutionary symbols. Local walnut, oak or fruitwood were used rather than imported mahogany, and combinations of metals.

230

Drop-leaf mahogany sofa table

Bamboo-turned
wood side chair

add an amusing accent to modern rooms.
Distinguishing features. Straight lines relieved
by simple but bold curves, well proportioned. Many
pieces were lacquered (usually black, white or
ivory) and highlighted with gold trim. Ornamentation was confined to metal inlays and applied
designs. Favored woods were rosewood, mahogany,
satinwood, with some exotics like ebony and holly.

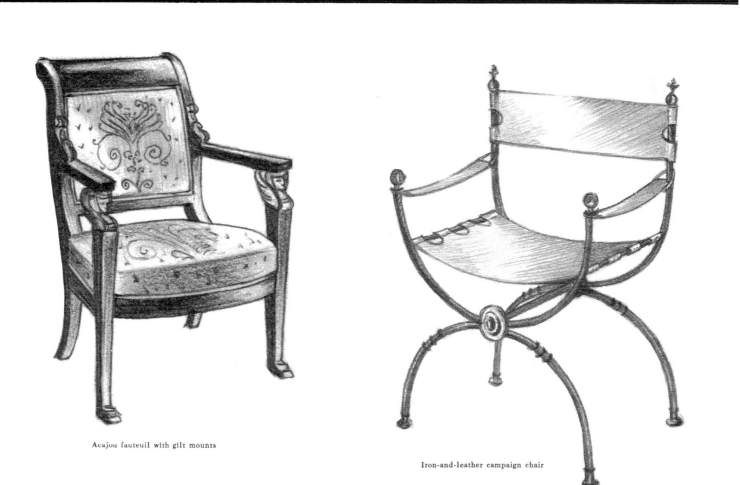

Acajou fauteuil with gilt mounts

Iron-and-leather campaign chair

231

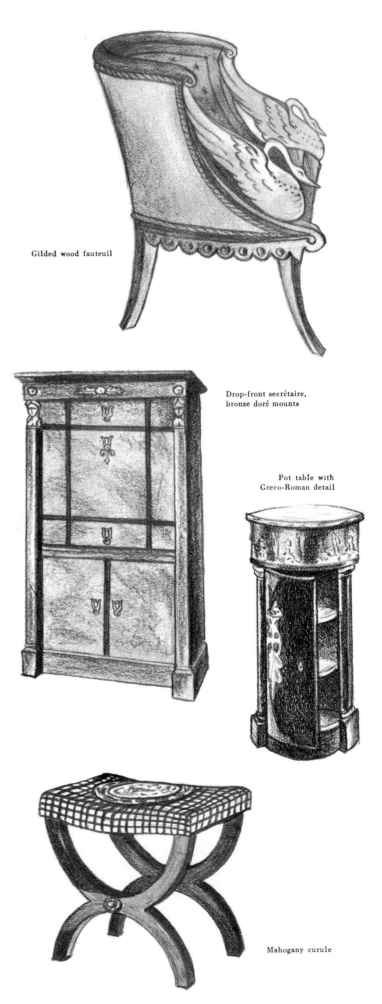

Gilded wood fauteuil

Drop-front secrétaire, bronze doré mounts

Pot table with Greco-Roman detail

Mahogany curule

FRENCH EMPIRE   1804–1815

Under Napoleon, the Directoire style became Imperial. At his command, Greek and Roman pieces were copied and adapted. The discriminating scale of Louis XVI and Directoire was debased, and furniture reached ponderous proportions, often ostentatiously ornamented with bronze and gilt appliqués. This style accommodated both massive architectural cabinets and the graceful Récamier chaise longue, the innovation of the period. Tables were circular, and supported by tripod or pedestal bases. Empire influences may be recognized in German Biedermeier, American Federal and English Victorian furniture.

Distinguishing features. Gross scale, motifs symbolic of the conquests of the Empire: Roman eagles, wreaths, torches, lions, sphinx, pineapple, the letter "N" framed in a victorious wreath, and another Napoleonic invention, the bee. Carving was seen only on arms, posts of chairs and table legs which often terminated in the shape of lions, griffins or human figures. Dark mahogany was the chosen wood and marble was highly approved.

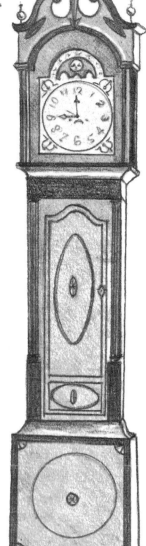

Serving table with pull-out shelves

Side chair with diamond lattice back

FEDERAL 1780–1830

The transitional era from the Revolution to Victorian-age America saw a welter of design influences, both imported and native. When peace was restored, the new English designs of Adam, Sheraton and Hepplewhite were adopted by American cabinetmakers, such as Samuel McIntyre of Salem, Massachusetts, who based his furniture on designs in Sheraton's book. After the French Revolution, an influx of émigré aristocrats resulted in a noticeable French influence on furniture, especially in the South. After the War of 1812, the mood of patriotism was capitalized on by American designers. The American eagle became the dominant motif, introduced in every conceivable manner from supports on chairs and tables to finials on mirrors and clocks and decorations painted on glass and china. The most important designer produced by this period was Duncan Phyfe, who set the pace for the other cabinetmakers. Even he succumbed to the decline of taste after 1830, and some of his later pieces, modeled after French Empire, are sadly clumsy and massive.

Tambour desk with inlays

BIEDERMEIER 1810–1850

Germany's early nineteenth-century equivalent of the French Empire style was in imitation of the grand houses of Paris. Woods were usually light or pale, pear and other fruitwoods, maple, birch, some mahogany. Period Biedermeier pieces with their admixture of sophisticated decoration and naive proportions are fashionable today as accents in contemporary rooms and are frequently reproduced in simplified, scaled-down versions.

Mahogany armchair with Directoire influence

DUNCAN PHYFE c. 1790–1856

The name of America's first great furniture designer has been immortalized in a style derived in part from English and French design of the period. His earliest work in Albany, New York, was in the manner of Adam and Hepplewhite. When he moved his workshop to New York, about 1790, he developed a trade in custom designs based on English Sheraton and French Directoire which has become known as American Federal. *Distinguishing features.* Lyre motif in chair backs and table bases. Mahogany was the preferred wood, but later pieces were made of rosewood.

Commode showing early
French Empire influence

Mahogany bed with French Empire influence

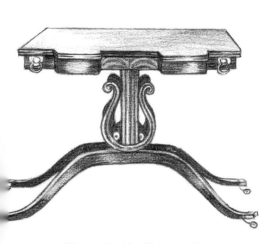

Flip-top side table with lyre motif

Open-arm chair showing classic influence

Mahogany serving chest

235

VICTORIAN

1835–1900

A style of nineteenth-century furniture—large, stalwart and often clumsy in appearance—developed from English and American Empire designs and generically named for Queen Victoria's long reign. Although many pieces have a quaint charm, the majority are poor examples of design. The Victorians, in a tireless search for what was novel, provoked revival after revival, virtually in caricature, with the result that this style mixes Gothic, Turkish, Egyptian, Venetian, Louis XV, as well as earlier Greek and Roman motifs. Later Victorian benefited from new machine processes that enabled such designers as Eastlake and William Morris to develop more functional pieces and a basic concept that is still good today. In this country the finest examples of Victorian are the work of Belter. Much furniture of the later Victorian period is still to be found in older houses and antique or secondhand furniture shops.

Distinguishing features. Soft curves combined with straight lines, exotic carving, turning, inlay of brass, wood, mother-of-pearl. Black walnut and rosewood predominate, with occasional pieces lacquered or made of papier-mâché.

English Victorian
Gothic armchair

American Empire sideboard
with tambour doors

English revolving bookstand

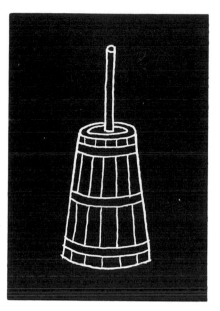

Pine storage cabinet

SHAKER

1776–1880

The Shakers, a self-sufficient religious sect of the mid-nineteenth century, made their own simple, straightforward furniture, mainly from pine, walnut, maple or fruitwoods. The very simplicity of the Shaker style has sustained it in popularity, but, because of its rarity, authentic pieces are quite expensive. The Shaker influence is strongly apparent in the unadorned functionalism of many of today's contemporary furniture designs.

John Belter rosewood gossip chair

Maple drop-leaf
sewing cabinet

Four-slat rail back rocker

237

MISSION
1895–1910

The early missions in California and the Southwest produced a style of furniture crudely but attractively fashioned of native materials by the Spanish missionaries and American Indians. Upholstery, generally leather, was studded with large nailheads. Ornamentation consisted of hand-hammered copper appliqués or simple cut-out patterns. By virtue of their sturdiness, many of the original pieces have survived, and today they are freely interpreted as part of the Spanish idiom. An unfortunate revival of Mission style in the 1900's, during the Arts and Crafts movement, saw pieces of heavy oak, finished with a dark, smoky stain, machine-made to simulate the original handcrafted mortise-tenon jointing.

Walnut table with turned legs, iron stretchers

ART NOUVEAU
1890–1910

During the late nineteenth century this form of decorative art which had been launched by Henri Van de Velde in Paris in 1895 spread throughout Europe and to the United States. Art Nouveau, which encouraged free but self-conscious interpretations of nature and was distinguished by imitative carving and undulating lines, encompassed styles derived from the Gothic and the Japanese (difficult to reconcile in combination). Examplars of the style are Van de Velde in Europe, Louis Comfort Tiffany in the United States. Unusual pieces that went out of fashion in the last generation and were banished to basements and attics are highly prized today.

Walnut armchair with tooled
leather back and sling seat

Walnut and wrought-iron
writing table

Double-pedestal desk with
bold flowing curves

Side chair with
naturalistic motifs

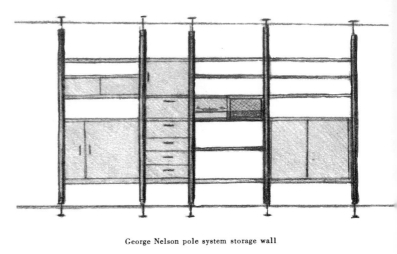

George Nelson pole system storage wall

CONTEMPORARY TWENTIETH CENTURY   From 1900

Until the Paris Exposition of Decorative Art in 1925, most furniture produced in the United States was nothing more than a parroting of the historical periods. The French Art Moderne inspired American designers to grapple with the idea of a modern style. Their first efforts resulted in a rash of geometric forms and exotic woods. Public reaction, a mixture of wonderment and ridicule, nevertheless opened the door to the acceptance of modern as we know it today. The Bauhaus school of Germany made outstanding contributions to contemporary design in plastics and metals, materials new to the market—the famous Barcelona chair is a classic example. Before World War II, Swedish Modern

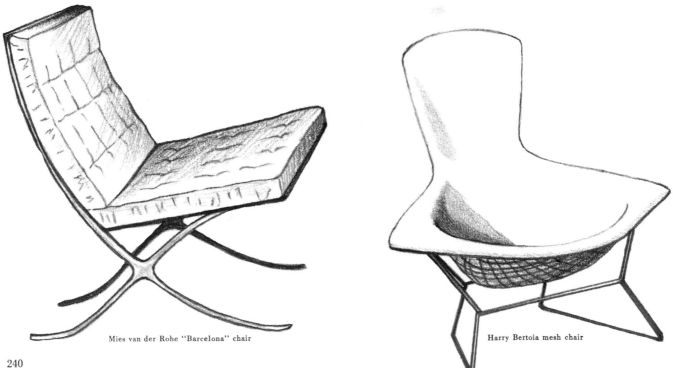

Mies van der Rohe "Barcelona" chair

Harry Bertoia mesh chair

240

Charles Eames lounge chair and ottoman

swept the country. The style owed something to Sheraton but was translated in simpler terms in blond mahogany. The Scandinavian school has remained the greatest producer of contemporary furniture for mass consumption, and American designers like Eames, Knoll, Saarinen and Nelson —all of whom have a firm foundation in architec- ture—have set a high standard of good contempo- rary design. Each year sees changes in the still transitional style. The general characteristics may be simply set forth as clean lines, elimination of inessential detail, adaptation of new materials, and functionalism which banishes any piece that does not pay its way in usefulness as well as beauty.

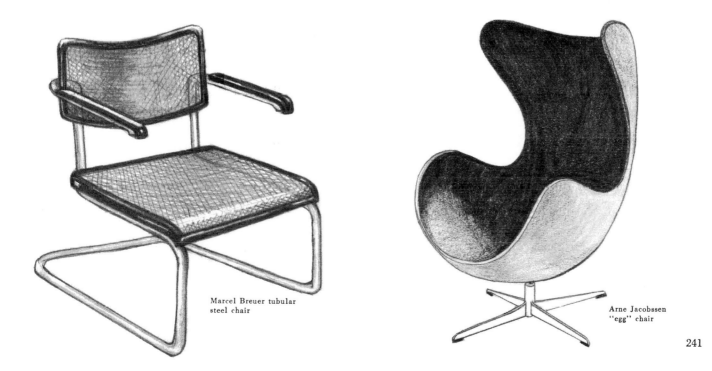

Marcel Breuer tubular
steel chair

Arne Jacobssen
"egg" chair

241

Decorating, like every art, has an idiom all its own.
Some of the words have been recently coined to dub
or to describe a current decorating trend, material or object.
The majority are holdovers from the past, particularly
the great periods of design and furniture making.

COMING TO TERMS

ALTHOUGH it is perfectly possible to grasp the principles of decorating without having a working knowledge of the language and a comprehension of what the different terms mean, it is quite another matter to discuss it with any degree of clarity. Professionals such as interior designers, architects and antique or furniture dealers are not being deliberately obscurantist when they prattle of distressed finishes and acoustical ceilings, semainiers and scagliola; they are only using the terms of their trade as any specialist does. And now that decorating styles have veered from the out-and-out modern to a mixture of styles and periods, you may well discover you have taken a duchesse into your bedroom or a marquise into your living room without resorting to Debrett. So, if you are at a loss to know the difference between a day bed and a sleigh bed (the former is not for daytime sleeping, nor the latter for cat naps in the snow—it merely has ends with curving, sleigh-like contours) or think that vargueño is a type of flamenco dancing, you may have some difficulty getting (or even knowing) what you want. This decorating glossary does not even attempt to cover the vast and specialized fields of antiques and collectors' items. It is simply intended as a guide to the terms most generally encountered and the new uses and applications that have been found for some of the more enduring antiques.

A

acanthus

A decorative motif adapted by the Greeks from the acanthus plant. Found in succeeding styles of design, in both bold and restrained versions,

A

accent

A catchall word which currently serves, in lieu of something more precise, to describe the element of contrast in a color scheme. As a noun or adjective, it usually refers to minor elements: pillows, paintings, slip covers, accessories, painted furniture. As a verb, it means to introduce a contrasting color or colors to a decorating scheme.

accent color

A color too vivid to be used lavishly or on a large scale, which adds a piquant note to a room when used in small controlled amounts.

accent rug

A small rug (below, left) designed to draw attention by its striking shape, color, texture or pattern, often seen under a coffee table or laid on top of wall-to-wall carpeting.

accessories

The changeable, decorative additions that round out a room scheme—lamps, clocks, pillows, art objects—as distinct from the major elements of decoration. Accessories add the personal stamp that makes a room more than a collection of furniture—and may, in some cases cost a great deal more than the furniture itself.

acoustical materials

Materials that absorb sound—acoustical tiles and acoustical plaster for ceilings and walls. Heavy draperies, fabric wall coverings, wall-to-wall carpeting and vinyl or cork tile floors, while not strictly acoustical materials, have similar noise-absorbing qualities.

advancing colors

A designer's term for warm colors such as red, orange and yellow which seem to bring a surface nearer—a visual illusion.

antique

U. S. Customs regulations define as antique anything made before 1830. This rather arbitrary classification is supposedly based on the year in which machine production, rather than handcraftsmanship, became customary. However, age is no guarantee of value or worth, and the status of an "antique" is more often determined by current attitudes and vogues—witness the recent upsurge of interest in Victorian and Art Nouveau, with a corresponding rise in price.

antiquing

The process or processes by which something new (chiefly wood or furniture finishes) is made to look old—simulated worm holes, worn-off edges, acid baths to give the appearance of age, glazes with washes of dirt tones to reduce the surface brilliance of painted finishes and suggest an uneven, old quality. Recently this phrase has acquired a secondary meaning: to go shopping for antiques.

apron

On furniture, the band of wood (with or without drawer) just under a table top, beneath the seat of a chair, along the base of a cabinet.

architectural interest

Term for simulated or real interior architecture such as beams, moldings, dadoes, paneling, added to a plain room (right). Many architectural effects today are clever copies of the real thing—structural papers or printed vinyls that simulate wood grain or brick, trompe l'œil versions of marble, plywood facsimiles of beams and wood paneling.

area rug

A small rug, 4 feet by 6 feet or over, larger than an accent rug but not as large as a room-size rug, often used to define one area of a room such as a dining or conversation group (below).

a

armoire

French version of a wardrobe; a piece of furniture traditionally used to store clothes, though the name may be derived from an earlier kind of storage, that of arms or armor. In America, with its plenitude of closets, armoires seldom hold clothes. Instead, they are much more likely to be converted into bars, stereo shelters or china closets.

Art Moderne

French term meaning modern or contemporary design. During the 1920's, a term used in the United States to describe the new breed of modern objects.

Aubusson

Hand-woven carpets or tapestries originating in the French town of Aubusson. The carpets are more valued today than the tapestries. Modern Aubusson carpets can be woven to order in any design, traditional or contemporary.

Austrian shade

Vertically shirred sheer curtains which are pulled up to any point like a shade, but with cords rather than a roller. Austrian shades were very popular a few years ago but, probably because they have become the standard window treatment for hotels and restaurants, the more tailored Roman shade seems to have taken over at home.

B

Baccarat

The crystal of the French kings, this exceptionally beautiful glass has been made in France from the early eighteenth century, and both old and modern pieces are highly prized by collectors. Cutting, pressing and blowing produce the patterns.

baluster

A small turned column, usually found as a support for a stair rail, now often a table or lamp base.

bamboo

Introduced during the eighteenth-century rage for things Chinese, the wood of the bamboo has for centuries been turned into furniture.

banquette

An upholstered bench, with or without a back.

batik

A hand-printed fabric, originally cotton, patterned by a process which involves dipping the cloth into a series of different-color dyes. Parts of the design not to be dyed any specific shade are made dye-resistant by a removable wax coating. Batik originated in the Dutch East Indies, and is now imitated in machine prints.

Belter

Victorian furniture made in New York after 1840 by John H. Belter and highly prized now for its excellent craftsmanship, fine carving and superb use of rosewood, walnut and oak.

b

bergère

An upholstered armchair with closed, upholstered sides developed in France during the eighteenth century. Unlike much period furniture the bergère is extremely comfortable, which explains its continuing popularity.

bibelot

A small decorative object of less value than an objet d'art but more than a trinket—in literal translation, a plaything.

bentwood

Wood softened by steam, afterward molded into shapely yet strong and inexpensive furniture—a nineteenth-century process which foreshadowed the twentieth-century laminates. Classic examples are the Windsor chair with its bow back and arms, and the chairs and rockers of the Austrian designer and manufacturer Thonet. Bentwood is currently enjoying a revival of interest, both in the contemporary designs of Alvar Aalto of Finland and reproductions of the old rockers and chairs, now frequently teamed in rooms with straight-lined modern furniture.

block front

A term applied to the front of a desk or chest which has three vertical panels, the center concave, the ends convex. Panel tops end in carved shells. Attributed to John Goddard of Newport, R.I.

248

boiserie

French word for the delicate eighteenth-century paneling and decorative woodwork, now loosely used to refer to any paneling.

bonheur du jour

A delightfully named, elegant little French lady's writing desk developed during the time of Louis XVI, which looks like a small cabinet with a drop front and slender curving legs. Still in fashion for small rooms because of its diminutiveness.

bombé

Term for furniture or objects with a surface that bulges or swells, either on the front, the sides or both, such as the commode above.

bonnetière

A tall, narrow cabinet designed in the eighteenth century for the singular function of holding the elaborate hats of the period. Today, elevated to the role of displaying books or decorative objects, it performs economically and most effectively on a short wall.

#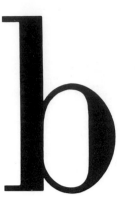

borax

Commonly used to describe a type of cheap, showy furniture with waterfall fronts, extraneous and tasteless ornamentation, and "printed" finishes. In the nineteenth century, manufacturers of the cleaning compound Borax offered premiums of furniture, which may well have inspired the name.

bouillotte

A Louis XVI circular game table, generally made of mahogany with openwork brass gallery and trim and marble top. An extra top or bouchon, one side covered with leather and the other with baize cloth, filled the space between marble and gallery for a playing surface. Today, few of these tables are used for games; most serve as lamp tables.

bouillotte lamp

The candle lamp of gilt bronze or brass with a painted tole shade that was set on or hung over the table was also called a bouillotte and, wired, is now a popular desk or table lamp.

Boulle

Inlay of brass in wood or tortoise shell identified in the work of Louis XIV's celebrated cabinet-maker André Charles Boulle.

bow front

The arched contour of the front of a chest.

burl

Also burr. A diseased or abnormal growth on trees, exalted to the status of a veneer wood when sliced into cross sections that show up the beautifully mottled or figured patterns.

C

cabriole

Serpentine curve of a furniture leg that swells outward at the knee, inward at the ankle, terminating at the foot in a short flare.

café curtains
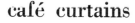

Tiers of short curtains hung, French café style, on rods at various levels so that they can be drawn open and closed to control light and view.

cane

A flexible rattan woven into patterns that has been a popular part of furniture, mostly chairs, since its first use in seventeenth-century England.

cartonnier

A businesslike piece of furniture with cardboard drawers designed for papers, the forerunner in eighteenth-century France of today's file cabinets.

case goods

The manufacturers' general term for storage pieces, as distinguished from upholstered seating pieces. Today, it may refer to dining room and bedroom pieces made predominantly of wood.

cassone

A large chest decorated with paint, inlays of carving, from Italy.

causeuse

French term—derived from the verb "to chat"—for a small upholstered settee, larger than a marquise but smaller than a canapé (period sofa).

chaise longue

A feet-up seating piece that can take various forms: an elongated chair or sofa with a chair back; a deep bergère extended by a matching upholstered stool; a pair of armchairs bridged by a stool.

chauffeuse

A small chair with low seat (rush or upholstered), designed for a vantage point at the fireside, child-size in scale but sturdy enough for adults.

C

chinoiserie

Popular French term in the eighteenth century for things Chinese or reminiscent in decoration of the Chinese fashion. Today, the word refers to painted or lacquered Chinese designs in furniture.

console

In effect, a wallflower in furniture. Any slim table or shelf designed for wall support. Usually a small table hung on the wall with curved or otherwise ornamental supports.

collection

A display of personal treasures such as paintings, sculpture, china, primitive art, objects with a similar theme or mementos.

commode

Succinct French word for a chest of drawers. The prim Victorians pre-empted the word to describe a stool or box which held a chamber pot.

conversation group

A scrupulous arrangement of furniture—chairs, sofas, benches, ottomans and small tables—planned to allow a number of persons to engage comfortably in conversation.

252

Creil

Glazed soft-paste pottery made in the French town of Creil-sur-Oise during the late eighteenth and early nineteenth centuries and ornamented with black stencil designs on one of three ground colors —white, canary yellow or water green (rare). Motifs were drawn from such assorted subjects as days of the month, military heroes or balloon ascensions. Since no Creil has been produced for many years, its rarity and distinctive character have made it a choice collectors' item.

conversation piece

Any object so decorative in itself, or in its placement in bold contrast to other pieces in the room, that it inspires comment and attention, such as the elaborate stove in the room above. Now widely used to refer to curiosities with nothing more than shock value that hardly merit house room.

crewel

A type of embroidery with colored worsted yarns and long loose stitches on cotton, linen or wool fabrics that had a tremendous vogue in the seventeenth century. Crewel in contemporary colors and motifs as well as the familiar traditional ones is now enjoying a revival.

cornice

A decorative crown, referring either to the top of a piece of furniture or, more generally, the finishing molding of a column or ornamental wood border installed above windows to conceal drapery and curtain rods and add a finishing touch.

cornice lighting

Striplights concealed behind a cornice or cove of wood in such a way that the light is directed upward to be reflected softly from the ceiling of a room, thus creating a sense of over-all illumination. Also called cove lighting.

Coromandel

The term for ebony from the Coromandel coast of India has become synonymous with a paneled screen (right) decorated with raised lacquer motifs, usually in deep tones of red, green or brown lacquer, sometimes soft ivory.

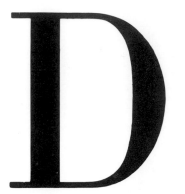

deal

The English term for pine, originally from the German word for plank.

denim

Anglicized from *serge de Nîmes* (Nîmes being the town in France where the fabric was first made), the word "denim" denotes a heavy twilled cotton sold by weight, usually yarn dyed and woven in twill (parallel or diagonal lines or ribs) and geometric figures.

distressed

Finish designed to age furniture prematurely, achieved through extreme measures that include beating with chains, stabbing with awls, shooting with beebees.

dry sink

A nineteenth-century cupboard with recessed well, lined in metal, for washing dishes. Water was brought to the dry sink since it had no plumbing connections, but today plants or a bar may be installed instead.

dado

The lower part of a wall topped by a chair rail, decorated with a panel of wood, paper or paint.

dual purpose

Term applied to a type of room or piece of furniture with twofold functions, for example, study-guest room, living-dining room, sofa-bed.

day bed

A bed treated as a sofa, with twin ends, to serve as a seating piece during the day. Or, alternately, a sofa that becomes a bed.

duchesse

Combination of an upholstered chair and ottoman, that pair up to form a couch or variation of a chaise longue, usually broad of seat and long on comfort.

E

ébéniste

French for cabinetmaker, from ébene (ebony), a favorite wood of cabinetmakers under Louis XIV.

eclecticism

The art of selecting the best from several sources, applied in decorating to an uninhibited mixture of styles of previous periods with designs of today.

encoignure

Corner piece or corner cupboard in French. Any piece that cuts corners to save space, gain storage, but not a large corner cupboard.

epergne

Table centerpiece made in graduated tiers of crystal, porcelain or metal, which may be used to hold flowers and fruit or bonbons.

escritoire

Writing desk (above, right) endowed with many little drawers, compartments and pigeonholes, one or more of which is a hidden cache. The secret compartment, in turn, gave the secretary its name.

étagère

A pyramid of open shelves (right) intended for the display of objects, better known in humbler circumstances, thanks to the Victorian era, as a what-not.

F

fauteuil

A French open-arm chair with either upholstered or caned seat and back, as distinguished from the completely upholstered bergère.

faux bois

Literally, false wood—a decorating deceit achieved through paint. The graining is usually exaggerated and need not necessarily duplicate actual wood tones.

festoon

A scallop-like garland or fillip that may be suggested either in fabric, looped and draped above a window, or in wood as a carved motif in furniture.

flock design

Raised design on fabric or wallpaper accomplished through felting, in imitation of the rich Venetian cut velvets.

focal point

A decorating element that dominates a room by virtue of its size or of the decorative treatment bestowed on it, to draw the eye in its direction. May be architectural (fireplace, built-in book or storage wall) or a piece of furniture like a breakfront, armoire, screen or a collection of art objects.

French polish

A shellac finish with a mirror gloss.

fringe

Upholstery or drapery trimming of loose threads which may be twisted, plaited and of silk, cotton, wool or combinations of materials.

fruitwood

Furniture wood from various fruit trees—pear, apple and cherry. Today, most fruitwood veneers are merely finishes that duplicate the color and grain of fruitwood.

functionalism

Furniture design determined by basic use rather than by decorative style.

G

gallery

Ornamental railing along the edge of a table, a shelf or a serving tray. The term also describes a long hall that is hung with paintings.

gazebo

An open, airy, even lacy, summerhouse or pavilion, often elaborately contrived. A popular vantage point in Victorian gardens, and in vogue again on today's terraces.

geometric print

A measured pattern based on triangles, circles, diamonds, etc., on fabrics and wallpapers, often taking the form of stripes, plaids, polka dots.

gesso

Raised decoration of plaster, projected in relief, for furniture, walls, architectural trim, usually further ornamented with paint or gilt.

gimp

Flat decorative tape used as a finishing trim to conceal upholstery tacks or stitching in draperies.

girandole

Word variously applied to a wall bracket with reflective mirror, sometimes referred to as bull's-eye.

glazing

Hard finish with a softening influence on the final coat of paint color. Shellac or varnish with added color is applied to a thin wash, then wiped off, to subdue the base color.

grille

Latticework of wood or metal in either simple crisscross geometric or more elaborate Moorish motifs. Employed as decorative obscuration in window panels, screens and room dividers, walls of buildings. Also a design printed on fabric or wallpaper to add dimensional quality.

g

grisaille

Decorative painting confined in color to tones of gray (*gris* in French). It usually depicts figures which appear in relief.

guéridon

Small round French table generally topped with marble, and used either as an occasional table or as a cocktail table.

H

hangings

Decoratively speaking, window or bed curtains or wall coverings such as tapestries. Originally used in medieval times to provide warmth and comfort.

hassock

Large overstuffed cushion upholstered to its base and used as a footstool or ottoman.

highboy

A tall chest of drawers, usually made in two parts: a table-like base with legs, and an upper chest. From *haut bois*, French for "high wood."

hunt table

A crescent-shaped or long sideboard table with drop leaves to extend the serving surface, designed for hunt breakfasts. The distinguishing feature is the height, tall enough for everyone to stand around it comfortably. With drawers, it was called a hunt board. Today, the semicircular hunt table is used as a buffet, a desk, or, lowered, as a coffee table.

hutch

Chest or cabinet on legs which supports an open-shelf deck. As a sideboard this was popular in early American households.

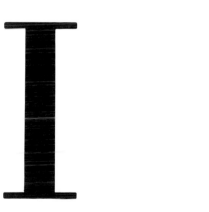

insert

A decorative inlay design formed by setting a shaped piece of one material into the surface of another. In flooring the word may refer to brass set in vinyl tile.

intarsia

The decorative forerunner of insert. Designs inlaid in wood through use of contrasting colors and textures of other woods, ivory, metal, tortoise shell or stones set flush with the surface.

japanning

A type of lacquerwork in which surfaces of wood or metal are coated with layers of varnish and then dried in heated ovens. May have high relief, incised or flat designs. A decoration borrowed from the Orient, it attained high excellence in France under Louis XIV and in England under Charles II. Today, japanning is rapidly becoming a lost art.

joint stool

Jacobean low stool, usually of oak and not upholstered, with turned and jointed legs. In today's liberal decorating lexicon the term may refer to an occasional table of this design.

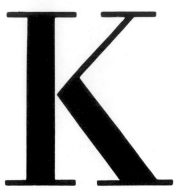

K

kas

Early American cabinet the size of an armoire, made by Dutch settlers. The wood may be walnut, pine, cherry or maple, and the kas is frequently carved, paneled or painted in primitive fashion with ornaments of fanciful flowers.

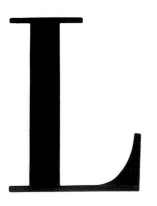

kd

Abbreviation for knock-down, a term for furniture that is designed in parts to be shipped unassembled, and put together by store or customer.

knotty pine

Pine where the knots are conspicuous. The twentieth-century vogue for knotty pine walls to simulate "Early American" is historically incorrect. Only clear pine, free from knots, was originally used, except where the surface was painted.

L

lambrequin

Shaped valance of fabric, bound or trimmed with fringe, which crowns a window, the top of a bed or a chair back.

laminates

Materials in lamination, a process in which thin layers of a given material are bonded to each other or to another material under great pressure. Plywood is a laminate, as are the plastics Formica and Micarta. The development of vinyl plastics gave new dimension to the process and made possible such aids to decorating as laminated fabric window shades, laminated cork and wood veneer floor tiles, laminated Japanese papers shaped into trays.

lavabo

Originally a functional piece of plumbing, the lavabo is a wall-hung wash basin in two parts (upper part is water container, lower part is basin) both of which are mounted on a wood back. Now used principally for decoration, often to hold plants.

lectern

A bookstand, originally ecclesiastical, made of wood, metal or stone.

linenfold

Carved paneling, originally Gothic, which represents the vertical folds of linen. May also have been inspired by the folded napkin on the chalice in church ritual.

lit clos

The French term for a bed enclosed on three sides with wood paneling. Provincial pieces of the eighteenth century are popular today in reproduction.

lit de repos

Lighthearted version of a day bed, designed for cat naps in the French fashion.

louvers

Slatted system to control light and air at windows or doors. Louvers may be vertical or horizontal, stationary or adjustable, wood, metal or plastic.

luminous ceiling

Installation of strip lights behind translucent panels which diffuse shadow-free light. Primarily used in kitchens, baths or windowless interior areas, and also as an ingenious device for creating a false ceiling in a room which is disproportionately high.

marbleizing

An artful painted finish that can make a wood or metal surface look for all the world like marble, except that the graining is apt to be exaggerated and the coloring more flamboyant.

marquetry

Veneers inlaid with contrasting materials (wood, ivory), but retaining a flat surface.

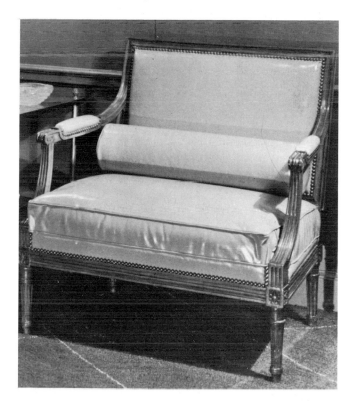

marquise

The French term for an armchair, very wide and completely upholstered, that was originally designed to accommodate panniered skirts.

m

mixing

Current cant for the popular pulling together in a single room of furniture and decorations of widely divergent periods, styles and countries.

molding

Raised, shaped strips of wood applied as decoration to plain walls, doors, fireplaces or furniture.

mosaic

Bits of wood, glass, stone, inlaid to form a design that may be pictorial or a conventional geometric.

motif

The predominant figure in a pattern or design repeated variously within a room. For example, a floral motif in curtains may be repeated on pillows or echoed in water colors or prints on a wall.

mounts

Metal fittings or decoration applied to furniture or objects. During the reign of Louis XV, bronze and gilt mounts supplied most of the decorative effects.

mullion

Slim divider to delineate glass panes in windows, In furniture it takes the form of tracery on glass doors of secretaries and bookcases.

muntin

The inside vertical dividers of a door or window frame used to mark the divisions between glass or wood panels of a door.

N

neoclassic

New interest or revival of interest in ancient cultures, as evidenced in the Renaissance, Adam and Empire styles which drew on classic motifs.

neutrals

The near colors or no colors—blacks, whites, grays, beiges, browns—usually considered punctuation or breathing space for other colors, particularly those of the four color families (red, yellow, blue, green). Wood tones are also embraced by the term, which may be paraphrased in fashion jargon as the "little nothing" colors.

objets d'art

Literally, objects of artistic worth; generally, accessories of important decorative value and, if not dear, difficult to come by.

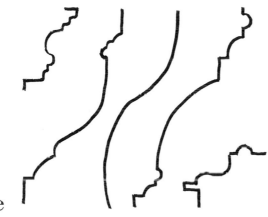

ogee

The side view or profile of a molding. The distinguishing line is a classic double-S curve or cyma.

opaline

Opalescent glass very popular in the nineteenth century and in favor again today. This type of translucent glass comes in lovely shades of blue, pink, green and white. Antique opaline is the pet of collectors and extravagantly priced.

open plan

Term used to describe a floor plan which banishes solid walls in favor of large open spaces. Kitchen, living room, dining room, study may be merely suggested in various ways by partial dividers, furniture arrangements, and so on.

Oriental rug

A type of rug hand-woven or hand-knotted, usually in elaborate designs. The number of borders determines the value. Origins may be Turkish, Chinese, Indian or Middle Eastern. Today, there are also machine-reproduced Oriental rugs.

ormolu

Golden pretenders in gilded brass, bronze or copper ornaments or mounts for furniture introduced by the French ébénistes of the eighteenth century.

ottoman

A luxurious perch that is nothing more than a low upholstered, backless, armless seat, reminiscent of the Turkish influence of the eighteenth century.

overscaled

Generously proportioned furniture or patterns of larger than usual size, deliberately scaled or composed for effect.

overstuffed furniture

Sofas and chairs that achieve a bumper effect because all wooden parts, with the exception of the feet, have been upholstered.

P

paisley

A fabric design in imitation of the woven Cashmere shawls, originally made at Paisley, Scotland —hence the name. Today, paisley designs are used in fabric and also printed on vinyl and wallpaper.

Palladian

The distinctive style of architecture which was Andrea Palladio's free interpretation of the classic orders, now applied to furniture which has a pleasing symmetry in its formality. England, Ireland and America enjoy the Italian's heritage in both architecture, notably that of the eighteenth century, and furniture designs.

panetière

This type of carved open box for the display of bread originated in France. Today, it is more often employed as an end table or enclosure for stereo.

papier-mâché

Paper, molded, glued and then lacquered, formed many articles in the seventeenth and eighteenth centuries. It was popular in Europe and America in the nineteenth century as a material for tables, boxes, side chairs and trays, which were usually black and embellished with inlays of mother-of-pearl in Oriental designs.

parquet

Geometric shapes of wood inlaid, mosaic fashion, for flooring and for furniture. Herringbone and other patterns distinguish parquet from marquetry.

patina

Mellowing of surface texture and color produced by age, wear and rubbing. So desirable is it that manufacturers take measures to fabricate the effect.

pedestal

A single—and singular—means of elevating chairs and tables without the support of legs. Architectural in design, the pedestal may divide when it reaches the table top or it may be solid as if the table were rising like a mushroom from the floor.

pediment

An architectural triangle over a portico, window, door or gable end of a house. The word applies in furniture to the top of a cabinet or high piece, as in Chippendale secretaries, broken or even rounded.

period furniture

Specifically, furniture made during the historical period or school for which it is named. Period design is frequently reproduced in another age, as Louis XVI was made in the nineteenth century.

pickling

Finish designed to change the complexion of wood. Originally, pickling was done by removing with vinegar the plaster base on painted wood. Now it is achieved by rubbing white paint into the grain of a light wood floor or furniture.

pietra dura

A design, often used for table tops, made by setting in mortar fragments of marble or semiprecious stones and then polishing the surface.

pilaster

An architectural conceit of an applied rectangular or half-round column to decorate a plain surface. Decorative rather than functional.

plate rail

Dado on a different level, the plate rail is a functional piece of architectural artistry that encourages the display of china above eye level and at a safe remove.

plinth

Derived from architecture, this term describes a block (square, round or even octagonal) of wood or stone employed as the base of a column, or, decoratively, as a pedestal for sculpture.

p

plywood

A process in which several thicknesses or plies of wood are glued together with the grain of one ply at right angles to the grain of an adjacent ply, an alternation of grains that produces a wood of greater strength than a solid wood. Plywood is made in two ways: veneer construction where several thicknesses of veneer are glued together; lumber core where thin layers of veneer are glued at right angles to a thick semi-porous core, the veneers being equal in number and thickness on both sides. Although plywood has been known for centuries, it is only in the last two decades that it has been used in quantity. Today, most flat areas of furniture are plywood.

pot table

The original night table, tubular in shape, with a door to conceal nighttime necessities and a marble top to hold the bedside oil lamp. Now used decoratively as an end table in a living room or in place of a pedestal to display statuary or sculpture.

polychrome

Literally, many colored. Generally, a term referring to furniture and objects which are painted and gilded, usually over gesso, to emphasize a design or to embellish a whole area with fantasies.

poudreuse

More popularly referred to as a vanity, this is a French powder table. The distinguishing feature is usually a mirror that raises in the mid-section.

pouf

Type of ottoman that is usually round and well upholstered, even button-tufted, to convey a look of comfort.

pre-Columbian

Arts and artifacts of the native Indian cultures of Mexico, Central and South America before the discovery of the New World by Columbus.

prie-dieu

Kneeler, now a chair with high back and low seat, and the additional advantage of a narrow shelf, rail or pad across the top which may be employed as an arm-rest or head-rest.

R

Récamier

French Empire chaise longue that resolves itself in a high curved end. Derived from a Roman couch, it was named for Madame Récamier who was immortalized by the painter David reclining on just such a piece.

receding colors

Cool colors like blue or green which, like sea and sky, seem to escape into the distance and therefore have the effect of making walls retreat.

redwood

This soft red-brown wood from the Pacific coast has great resistance to decay and insects and weathers well—hence its use for siding on houses and outdoor furniture. Recently it has also become popular for interior paneling.

rafraîchissoir

An elegant ancestor of the bar cart, this Louis XV serving table was primarily intended for chilling wine, and to this end had a top fitted with tole or iron bottle holders. Under-shelves held extra dishes and glasses. Today, these practical little walnut or fruitwood tables are mostly used as decorative end tables, and the wells, instead of chilling wine, flaunt plants or flowers.

random pattern

An artfully aimless design conceived irregularly rather than as a formal repeat. In wallpaper, a random pattern, scattered instead of spaced in set limitations, may be applied successfully to camouflage jogs and beams on walls and ceilings.

refectory table

Originally a long narrow table built close to the floor and supported by heavy stretchers. When this kind of table was later shortened and fitted underneath with pull-out leaves, it became the first self-contained extension table.

r

repoussé

Decorative sheet metal work. The design is projected in relief on the front through hammerings from the back.

reproductions

Copies of old pieces, faithful in duplication of all details and even in finish and patina. Today, the word "reproduction" may be applied more loosely to commercial pieces that have some of the flavor, if not the accuracy, of the original because materials and proportions have been changed.

rococo

A style of decoration predominant in eighteenth-century Europe, in particular during the reign of Louis XV, in which rocailles (rocks), coquilles (shells) and similar motifs borrowed from nature were translated into a profusion of carved and painted ornaments. The motifs appeared in interior decoration, applied asymmetrically rather than in the symmetrical balance of the classic styles.

Roman shade

A neat variation on the Austrian shade in which the folds of the flat fabric panel are horizontally accordion-pleated rather than being shirred in scallops, giving a much more tailored effect.

room divider

Improvised partition to separate areas of a room. May be free-standing or built-in—a storage wall, sliding panels, a piece of furniture or as simple a device as curtains on a track or a folding screen.

scagliola

Hard plaster substance imbedded with small pieces of granite, marble, alabaster and other stones, and highly polished. Used for chest or table tops.

scale

Size and proportion of a piece relative to its surroundings and to other pieces in a room. Furniture with slim low lines earns the term "light-scaled"; whereas that which is large and massive would be considered heavy in scale.

sconce

A wall bracket that is decorative and dispenses light, originally in the form of a candle or oil lamp, today electrified for smokeless light.

semainier

A tall narrow chest of drawers developed during the reign of Louis XV and so named because it contained seven drawers, one for each day of the week. Modern reproductions of this piece are made today in several versions, some with only six drawers.

serpentine front

The sinuous shape of a commode, chest or bureau that curves inward at the ends and outward at the center.

set off

Decorating tactic to achieve visual definition or distinction, as the use of vinyl tile might set off a dining area from a carpeted living area.

settee

Long seat or bench with open arms and back, sometimes upholstered, sometimes caned.

settle

All-wood settee with solid arms and back, usually built like a box, solid to the floor, with hinged seat. The words "settee" and "settle" are often confused, perhaps because the latter is more pleasing.

sheer

Transparent or translucent fabric, thin and lightweight, frequently selected for curtains to admit diffused light.

shoji

Japanese term for wood-framed translucent sliding panels used as room partitioning.

S

show wood

Exposed wood parts of an upholstered piece of furniture—a chair or sofa—frame, leg, apron.

silicone finish

Colorless protective finish that endows the most fragile fabric with an iron constitution, repelling stains, liquids, dirt. Known by brand names like Scotchguard and Syl-mer.

soffit

The underside of a projecting cornice, beam or wide molding. Often a concealment for lighting.

soupière

Soup tureen with cover and platter. In furniture the soupière in the form of a vase is found in Louis XVI and Empire pieces, pedimented tops of beds, cabinets, chairs and at intersection of stretchers.

splat

The central vertical member of a chair back, the treatment of which is often indicative of a style of furniture, as the scrolled splat of Queen Anne.

270

spoon back

A chair "spooned" or shaped to complement the contour of the human body; specifically a Queen Anne chair.

spatterdash

A textured, flecked effect achieved in painted floor finishes by tapping a paintbrush with a stick or over a block of wood, and reproduced ready-made in vinyl tile.

spindle back

Chair back in a series of slender vertical turned members, most often applied to Windsor chairs. Popular since the seventeenth century.

stylized

Designed according to the rules of style rather than the vagaries of nature. A stylized floral design is characterized by a precise, formal pattern.

suite

A complete set of matched furniture, at one time admirably conceived (as in the eighteenth century), but in our time more often an unimaginative and undesirable group of inexpensive furniture.

swag

A decoration representing hanging drapery, ribbons, garlands of fruit and flowers. A window may be crowned with a decorative fabric drape caught up at the ends.

T

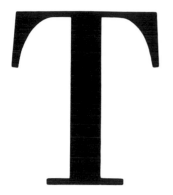

tabouret

Drum-shaped stool or seat, without arms or back, used as a stand or end table.

tambour

Flexible slatted door fronts on furniture that operate either vertically or horizontally. Thin strips of wood are glued to linen or duck and installed in a groove that may follow any contour. Tambour also refers to modern machine embroidery made to resemble handwork done on a tambour frame.

terrazzo

A poured cement floor in which marble chips are imbedded, then polished to a smooth high gloss.

tête-à-tête

Polite conversation piece of the nineteenth century, the tête-à-tête is a small love seat for two or three, with seats facing in opposite directions.

tête de nègre

Literally, the head of a Negro, but in decoration, a deep black-brown color with a touch of purple.

textural interest

Variations in surfaces throughout a room to add interest, particularly when the color scheme is monochromatic. Wood, brick, caning, fieldstone, grasscloth and split bamboo are much used.

ticking

A heavy, strong cotton fabric woven in stripes, patterns or plain, and originally used to cover mattresses. Now its sturdiness and hard-wearing qualities have made it popular for wall coverings (applied like paper), slip covers and curtains.

tie-back

Cord, fabric bands or ornamental devices for holding straight curtains back at the sides.

Tiffany glass

Fantastically colored iridescent glass produced by Louis Comfort Tiffany at the turn of the century and also called "Favrile," meaning hand-made. Recently returned to fashion, the most collected Tiffany glass pieces are the vases, distinguished by unusual flowerlike forms with surfaces of swirling color, the fancifully designed leaded glass shades and table lamps and the glass tiles in exotic patterns derived from the Near East.

t

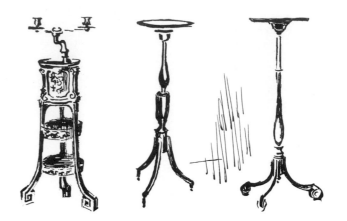

toile de Jouy

"Toile" is the euphonious French word for a finely woven cotton fabric, and a toile de Jouy is the same fabric printed with classical scenes, usually in one color on a white or off-white ground, from the French town of Jouy. These charming cotton prints were introduced in the eighteenth century and have been favorites ever since.

tole

Shaped and painted tin or metalware used for decorative objects like lamps, chandeliers, trays, occasional tables, boxes.

torchère

A portable stand for lights, originally a stand to hold a great candelabra in France.

transition

A smooth progression from one thing to another that constitutes an important aspect of decoration because open planning has all but banished doors. An entrance hall may be decorated in a way that provides a transition from the decoration of the living room to that of the dining room.

trapunto

Quilting that may either outline a printed pattern or create design interest on a plain fabric.

travertine

Type of stone with open-grain surface texture used, like marble, for flooring, table tops.

triptych

The three parts implied by the term may refer to a hinged mirror or screen or to paneled altar pieces that came to be used decoratively.

trivet

A three- or four-legged metal stand or table originally used for warming dishes by the fire, now promoted to plant stand or occasional table.

trompe l'œil

In translation from the French, "to fool the eye," this expression is applied to an ancient art form that does just that—makes things appear other than they are. Paint or paper can simulate dimension, architecture or a view. Today, wallpapers simulate marble, wood, tile, paneling and even three-dimensional objects.

trumeau

French word for a combination mirror with a painting over it. In the Louis XV and XVI periods, this was built into the overmantel or into the paneling between two windows. Today, it is more often seen as a hanging mirror.

unify

To blend visually disparate or unrelated furnishings in a room through the use of a single color family or fabric.

used furniture

Strictly second-hand furniture. Not to be confused with antiques, even though some self-styled antique dealers have developed a knack for making anything old, if not valuable, look chic.

valance

Shaped wood, stamped or pierced metal, draped, gathered or straight fabric used across the top of a drapery treatment or a canopied bed.

vargueño

A Spanish drop-front cabinet desk of the sixteenth, seventeenth and eighteenth centuries which was set on a separate base, either a table or chest. Cabinet contains many drawers, and has handles on sides for transporting. The pieces could be used together or independently.

veneer

A thin layer of decorative wood bonded to solid, less glamorous wood surfaces to impart strength and beauty.

Venetian

An eighteenth-century style of furniture developed from the rococo by the Venetians, who had a high regard for the ornamental and created fancifully painted pieces with theatrical profiles. The most highly regarded today are those based on Louis XV and Louis XVI styles.

vermeil

Gilded silver or bronze developed originally as a substitute for solid gold. To replenish their depleted treasuries, the spendthrift kings of France confiscated gold services and objects from their unlucky subjects—hence the demand for vermeil which reproduced the look of gold at a fraction of the cost, without sacrificing quality or detail. Now valued in its own right as an elegant, luxurious step-up from silver.

vernis Martin

A varnish finish of great brilliance and depth, but less durable than lacquer, attributed to the Martin brothers during the reign of Louis XIV. Oriental lacquer was the inspiration.

vitrine

A combination display and storage piece for china and objets d'art. The French word describes a cabinet with glass doors and sometimes a glass top and sides as well.

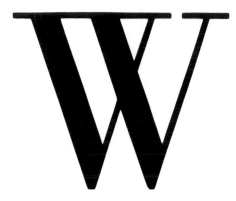

wainscot

Geometrically designed wall paneling that stops short of the ceiling, sometimes terminated by a plate rail. Popular in Tudor and Victorian homes.

wall covering

A term that encompasses all the materials other than paper used today, on walls—grasscloth, tile, adhesive-backed felt, paper-backed fabric, vinyl.

wardrobe

A portable closet for clothes; an armoire.

Waterford

Fine quality cut glass produced since the eighteenth century in Waterford, Ireland, and world-renowned for exquisite chandeliers, sconces and goblets.

Welsh dresser

A cabinet that begins as an enclosed storage piece, which is the base, and develops into a set-back upper part composed of open shelves.

wicker

Generic term for an airy, woven furniture material of various natural or synthetic fibers like willow, reed, rattan or twisted paper.

Windsor chair

Named for Windsor Castle in England and introduced during the reign of Queen Anne, Windsor chairs achieved their greatest prominence and most graceful styling in America from 1725 to 1800. The original chairs were made by wheelwrights who laced the bentwood back frames with spindles for support and pegged legs into saddle-shaped seats. Variations in shape include the hoop, the comb, the fan, the bow, the braced and the rocker. Still a favorite style and much reproduced.

DECORATION U.S.A. *acknowledges with appreciation the co-operation and contributions of the following architects, interior designers, decorative resources and photographers.*

ARCHITECTS AND INTERIOR DESIGNERS

DECORATIVE RESOURCES

Albano Company, Inc.

B. Altman & Company, New York

American-Standard

American Telephone & Telegraph

American Viscose Corporation

Amtico

Arco Lighting, Inc.

Baker Furniture, Inc.

David Barrett Inc.

Bess Bernard Interiors

Biggs Antique Furniture Company

Charles Bloom Inc.

Bloomingdale's, New York

Jacques Bodart, Inc.

Louis W. Bowen, Inc.

Churchill J. Brazelton Antiques

Herbert Bright, Inc.

Brunschwig & Fils Inc.

The Brunswick Corporation

Yale R. Burge, Inc.

Cabin Crafts, Inc.

Caledonian Inc.

Celanese Corporation of America

Clavos, Inc.

Colonial Mfg. Company

Doris Dessauer, Inc.

Devenish of London Inc.

Directional Furniture Inc.

Dunbar Furniture Corp.

Tom Durkin Antiques

Dux Inc.

Erwin-Lambeth Inc.

Fiberesin Plastic Company

Ficks-Reed Company

Fieldcrest Mills Inc.

Edward Fields, Inc.

Formica Corporation

General Tire & Rubber Company

Greeff Fabrics Inc.

Hacienda Furniture

Fritz Hansen, Inc.

The S. M. Hexter Company

Howard & Schaffer Inc.

Interchemical Company

Kentile Inc.

Kindel Furniture Company

Kittinger Company Inc.

Knoll Associates

Samuel Kootz Gallery

Laverne Originals

Lehigh Furniture Corp.

Jack Lenor Larsen, Inc.

Lord & Taylor, New York

Lozano-Fisher Studios, Inc.

The Magee Carpet Company

The Magnavox Company

Karl Mann Associates

Martin-Senour Paint Company

McGuire Furniture Company

Midtown Gallery

Herman Miller, Inc.

Milling Road Shop

Molla, Inc.

Museum of Contemporary Crafts

Old Stone Mill Corp.

Orchard House

Margaret Owen, Inc.

Owens-Corning Fiberglas Corp.

Florian Papp, Inc.

Parkwood Laminates, Inc.

Parzinger Originals, Inc.

Pittsburgh Plate Glass Company

Peter Prince, Inc.

Harvey Probber, Inc.

Jens Risom Design, Inc.

Roundtree Country Reproductions, Inc.

Rhoda Sande

F. Schumacher & Company

Selig Mfg. Company

Simmons Company

W. & J. Sloane, New York

Southwood House

Stark Carpet Company

John Straus, VKG

George Tanier, Inc.

Telescope Folding Furniture Company

Tile Council of America

Tomlinson of High Point, Inc.

Union Carbide Chemicals Company

United States Plywood Corp.

U. S. Rubber Company

Venetian Blind Institute

John Vesey, Inc.

V'Soske, Inc.

Wallpaper Council Inc.

Western Pine Association

Westinghouse Electric Corp.

Widdicomb Furniture Company Inc.

Willow & Reed Inc.

Window Shade Mfg. Association

Lee L. Woodard Sons

Wunda Weve Carpet Company

PHOTOGRAPHERS

ARTISTS